Decades of our Lives

80s

Decades of our Lives

CLASSIC, RARE AND UNSEEN 80s

FROM THE ARCHIVES OF THE DAILY MAIL

Trans
Atlantic
Press

Ronald Reagan and Margaret Thatcher formed a powerful right-wing axis in the West, while Mikhail Gorbachev's ascendancy to the Soviet premiership ushered in a new era of openness. The Cold War thawed, Communist-bloc countries turned away from Moscow and the Berlin Wall came crashing down. The desire for greater democracy reached China, where a lone student faced down a line of tanks during protests that were ruthlessly quelled. Britain and Argentina went to war over the Falkland Islands, while the West backed Saddam Hussein's Iraq in its conflict with neighboring Iran. Capitalism came under the microscope in a period that became synonymous with acquisitiveness. The 'haves" were exhorted to part with some of their cash as Bob Geldof pricked the world's conscience over the starving of Ethiopia. If Live Aid was the entertainment event of the decade, the society equivalent was the fairytale wedding of Prince Charles and Lady Diana Spencer. There were many disasters to contend with: Chernobyl, Zeebrugge, Lockerbie, Hillsborough, Heysel, the Challenger space shuttle; HIV hit the headlines as a new killer disease. Sport provided numerous uplifting moments, including Coe's Olympian feats, Maradona's World Cup wizardry and Torvill and Dean's *Bolero* magic.

From the momentous and the apocalyptic to the offbeat and the trivial, the photographs in this book, from the archives of the *Daily Mail*, chart the people, places and events that made up a memorable decade.

1980

Iranian demonstrators praying in London
the day after six armed terrorists seized
control of the Iranian Embassy there.
The terrorists were Iranian separatists
demanding the release of political prisoners
held in Iran following the previous year's
Islamic Revolution.

7

1980

LEFT: The press first began to realize a friendship was developing between Lady Diana Spencer and Prince Charles in the fall of 1980. After she was invited to visit the Prince and the royal family at Balmoral, Diana returned to London to find photographers camped on her doorstep and at the kindergarten where she worked. She was no stranger to the royal family, her first home being Park House in the grounds of Sandringham, the royal residence in the east of England. Her maternal grandparents had been great friends of King George VI and the Queen Mother, and some of her childhood playmates were Prince Andrew and Prince Edward.

OPPOSITE: Prince Charles pictured on a trek in the foothills of the Himalayas. Thereafter his route would be known as the Royal Trek. The Prince's strong relationship with Nepal had been cemented when he became Colonel-in-Chief of the Gurkhas (the legendary Nepalese brigade of the British army) in 1977.

1980

OPPOSITE: Bjorn Borg falls to his knees in celebration of his dramatic victory over John McEnroe (right) in the Men's Singles final at Wimbledon. The Swede won his fifth successive Wimbledon title after an arduous four-hour, five-set match at the All England Club.

1980

LEFT: President Saddam Hussein of Iraq welcomes Yasser Arafat, Chairman of the Palestine Liberation Organization, to Baghdad soon after the outbreak of the Iran–Iraq War. The PLO tried to mediate a ceasefire between the two countries and refocus their attention on the Arab–Israeli conflict.

OPPOSITE: Czechoslovakian-born British press baron Robert Maxwell, who rose from poverty to build an extensive publishing empire. Following his death under mysterious circumstances in 1991, his empire collapsed, revealing many financial irregularities, including the misuse of the company pension fund.

1980

OPPOSITE: Undisputed Middleweight Champion "Marvelous" Marvin Hagler took the title away from Alan Minter after a technical knockout in the third round of their fight at Wembley Stadium in London. The fight ended in chaos when a riot broke out after Hagler was acclaimed champion.

RIGHT: Fitness for all: the keep fit craze at the start of the decade reaches the House of Commons gymnasium.

1980

In Lake Placid, New York, with 10 minutes to play in the Olympic ice hockey semi final, the US team took the lead over their opponents from the Soviet Union, winning through to the final at the 1980 Winter Olympics. Jubilation ran high in the closing moments of the game, with the score 4–3. The Soviet team was acknowledged to be the best in the world while the US team was raised from college and amateur sides, however with Cold War tensions still in the air, the US team gave their all, going down in history with the match that was dubbed "The Miracle on Ice." This took them on to win gold in the final against Finland.

1980

gasolio

ABOVE: A porter recreates the shooting of J.R. Ewing with actor Larry Hagman. "Who shot J.R.?" fever spread around the globe and Hagman, who played the villainous character in the top-rated TV show *Dallas*, even made a promotional visit to Scotland Yard to see whether they had any leads. A record number of Americans tuned in to the November 1980 episode that finally unmasked his sister-in-law-cum-mistress as the assailant.

OPPOSITE: Devastation caused by the earthquake that took place in the Irpinia region in southern Italy on November 23, 1980. Measuring 6.89 on the Richter Scale, the quake centered on the village of Conza, killed 2,914 people, injured more than 10,000, and left 300,000 homeless.

1980

LEFT: Cast members of the George Lucas movie *Star Wars Episode V: The Empire Strikes Back*. Pictured from left to right: Mark Hamill, Carrie Fisher, Peter Mayhew, and Harrison Ford. Making his fellows look tiny, Mayhew, who played Chewbacca, was 7 feet 3 inches tall. This first sequel to the original 1977 movie was a great financial success, even though it was one of the most expensively made film of its day. Although now widely regarded as the best film in the *Star Wars* saga, critics gave mixed reviews on its release.

OPPOSITE: Lloyd Bridges and Robert Stack starred in the satirical comedy *Airplane!*, a clever spoof of disaster movies. The lead actors were not noted as comedy actors, which added to the hilarity of the writing and the gags. The film was nominated for a Golden Globe Award in 1981 for Best Motion Picture and remains a much-loved comedy classic around the world.

ABOVE: George Cole and Dennis Waterman in the long-running TV crime series with a touch of comedy, *Minder*. Following a formula about the British petty-criminal underworld, the two protagonists are "dodgy" but not dangerous, unless really bad guys start to try something on. In which case, Terry comes out of his corner in full fighting mode.

OPPOSITE: American actor Martin Sheen starred in Francis Ford Coppola's 1979 movie *Apocalypse Now*, which received a Palme d'Or at Cannes, two Oscars and a further six nominations. The picture gained Sheen wide recognition but he was lucky to survive a heart attack during filming in the Philippines in 1977. *The Final Countdown*, a far-fetched sci-fi movie, was Sheen's next film, released in 1980.

OPPOSITE: Canadian singer-songwriter, poet, and novelist Leonard Cohen shares a joke over a a cigarette. Cohen's song "Hallelujah," released on the 1984 album *Various Positions*, would bring him back to mainstream fame 20 years later when it was a posthumous hit for Jeff Buckley.

RIGHT: Artist David Hockney, giant of the Pop-Art movement, was a native of Yorkshire in the north of England but found his keynote inspiration in California, first making his name in the 1960s with a series of paintings based around swimming pools.

OPPOSITE: Post-punk/New Wave band Adam and the Ants released "Antmusic" in December 1980. The single reached number two in the British charts, kept off the top spot by "Imagine," which was re-released in the aftermath of John Lennon's murder. Developing a distinctive dress style, they applied their visual impact to video and were one of the first bands to exploit the music video as a platform.

LEFT: The clock face of London's most famous landmark, Big Ben, gets a spring clean.

LEFT: The 1980 movie *Victory* saw Sylvester Stallone (pictured) and Michael Caine as Allied POWs forced to compete in a soccer match against a German team in Nazi-occupied Europe. The Hollywood stars teamed up with some of soccer's greatest stars including Bobby Moore, Ossie Ardiles, and Pelé.

OPPOSITE: Arsenal's Liam Brady goes for goal as West Ham's Trevor Brooking and Ray Stewart close in during the 1980 FA Cup final tie at Wembley, London. West Ham won the match 1–0.

1980

Dan Aykroyd and John Belushi of The Blues Brothers perform in August 1980 at the Universal Amphitheater, Los Angeles, where they recorded their third album, *Made in America*. The Blues Brothers started life in 1978 as a skit on TV show *Saturday Night Live,* parodying other Blues acts. The Blues Brothers proved popular and the band started to play live venues and then made the Hollywood movie of the same name in 1980, which proved a classic comedy. Like the cameo performances by famous names in the movie, the band would rotate its line-up, with well-known artists playing instruments; the varying line-up was even more of a necessity after Belushi's untimely death in 1982.

1980

RIGHT: Actress Loretta Swit meets Kermit the Frog and Miss Piggy on *The Muppet Show*. Swit played Margaret "Hot Lips" Houlihan on the top-rated Korean War comedy *M*A*S*H*.

OPPOSITE: John Travolta starred in *Urban Cowboy* opposite Deborah Winger in 1980. He played Bud Davis, a country boy from Texas who moves to the city where he meets and marries a girl named Sissy (Winger). The film is credited with kick-starting a resurgence in the country music industry in the 1980s.

OPPOSITE: Steve Davis caused a sensation by reaching the quarter-finals of the World Snooker Championship in 1980 and by going on to win the UK Championship in the same year. The 22-year-old player would dominate the sport in the 1980s, picking up six World Championship titles between 1981 and 1989.

LEFT: At just 15 years old, American tennis player Andrea Jaeger reached the quarter-finals at Wimbledon in 1980, beating former champion Virginia Wade along the way.

EMBASSY WORLD SNOOKER

ABOVE: Iraqi President Saddam Hussein visits a kindergarten to try to convince the Iraqi public that it is business as usual, despite the war with Iran. In reality the war was a punishing conflict lasting eight years and taking half a million lives, with many more casualties.

OPPOSITE: Robert Mugabe's ZANU movement won Zimbabwe's first post-independence elections in February 1980 and Mugabe became Prime Minister. His government brutally suppressed opposition among the Ndebele people of the Matabeleland in western Zimbabwe in what is widely considered to be genocide. Here, Mugabe meets with Britain's Foreign Secretary Lord Carrington to discuss British concerns that Mugabe's men were using violence and intimidation against political opponents.

OPPOSITE: Britain's Sebastian Coe crosses the finish line in the men's 1,500 meter final at the Olympic Games in Moscow. The USA and a number of other nations boycotted the games in response to the Soviet invasion of Afghanistan.

RIGHT: Britain's Duncan Goodhew loosens up on the poolside. He picked up a gold and a bronze in the pool for 100 meter breaststroke and 4 x 100 meter medley respectively.

1980

ABOVE: President Jimmy Carter sits on his desk in the Oval Office as he meets with members of his cabinet to discuss the Iranian hostage crisis. Fifty-three Americans were held hostage for 444 days from November 4, 1979, to January 20, 1981, after a group of Islamist students and militants took over the American Embassy in Tehran in support of the Iranian Revolution. In April 1980 Carter authorized Operation Eagle Claw—the rescue attempt which failed badly, resulting in the deaths of eight US military personnel and the loss of a Hercules refueling aircraft and six helicopters.

OPPOSITE: In the case of the Atlanta Child Murders, at least 29 black children, adolescents, and adults were murdered over a two year period. Here two people are pictured searching woodland around Atlanta. A number of victims were found in woodland but the murders did not fit a clear pattern in every case, although strangling or asphyxiation was a common cause of death. Twenty-two-year-old Wayne Williams was tried and convicted for two of the murders but after his incarceration murders with similar pattern occurred in the Atlanta area, implying either copycat killings or that the true killer had not been captured.

George Brett of the Kansas City Royals bats against the Philadelphia Phillies during the World Series at Royals Stadium in Kansas City, Missouri, in October 1980. Although the Royals lost the series to the Phillies 4–2, they had won the American League West, helped by Brett's outstanding batting average, which won him the accolade of MVP (Most Valuable Player) from the American League that season.

1980

ABOVE: Irish-born actor Pierce Brosnan in the 1980 British drama-documentary *Murphy's Stroke;* he also made his movie debut in *The Long Good Friday* in the same year. Before his international breakthrough role as James Bond, Brosnan won fame in the USA, appearing in the TV detective series *Remington Steele*.

OPPOSITE: Jack Nicholson in Stanley Kubrick's psychological horror movie, *The Shining*. Despite mixed reviews at its release, the film is now hailed as one of the best horror films of all time, reaching iconic status for its surreal imagery.

1980

World Lightweight Champion "Sugar" Ray Leonard throws a punch at Roberto Duran during their fight at the Forum in Montreal, Canada, on June 20, 1980, dubbed "the Brawl in Montreal" by *Sports Illustrated*. Duran won on points at the end of a close-fought 15-round match, regaining the world title. However, Duran's success was short-lived: in November Leonard won the rematch in New Orleans with Duran retiring in the seventh round.

...SUBSTANTIATES THAT LENNON'S KILLER DID NOT ACT ALONE!! (SEE BELOW!)
WAS KILLED ONE WEEK BEFORE A SCHEDULED APPEARANCE IN A LABOR STRIKE!

JOHN LENNON'S MURDER WAS A POLITICAL ASSASSINATION!

IT WAS BY NO ACCIDENT OR WHIM THAT JOHN LENNON'S ASSASSINATION CAME AT PRECISELY THE POINT WHEN LENNON RE-EMERGED INTO PUBLIC AND POLITICAL LIFE AFTER 5 YRS. OF SECLUSION FOLLOWING ATTEMPT TO DEPORT HIM!

ASSASSINATION INFORMATION COMMITTEE

LENNON ASSASSINATION WAS PART OF A PATTERN WITH CWP-5, MILK & MOSCONE, LOWENSTEIN, GARCIA, etc. AS U.S. GOVERNMENT ESCALATES PREVENTIVE ELIMINATION OF OPPOSITION!

JOHN LENNON'S ASSASSINATION WAS A CASE OF PREVENTIVE ELIMINATION OF POTENTIAL OPPOSITION AND AN ATTEMPT TO INTIMIDATE & DEMORALIZE THE MASSES WHO IDENTIFIED WITH LENNON AND THE ANTI-WAR MOVEMENT AS THE ROCKEFELLER-LED U.S. CAPITALIST CLASS & ITS SECRET POLICE (LED BY THE CENTRAL INTELLIGENCE AGENCY) SEEK TO PROMOTE A RIGHTWARD SHIFT IN U.S. POLITICS IN ORDER TO COUNTERACT THE NATURALLY OCCURRING LEFTWARD SHIFT COMING ON THE HEELS OF THE MUTINY OF U.S. SOLDIERS IN VIETNAM (BLACKED OUT IN ALL MEDIA), THE HEROIC VICTORY OF THE VIETNAMESE PEOPLE OVER U.S. CAPITALISM-IMPERIALISM, THE WATERGATE PERIOD, AND THE WIDESPREAD RECOGNITION OF THE ECONOMIC-SOCIAL-POLITICAL FAILURES OF CAPITALISM! DOMESTICALLY AND WORLDWIDE!

"IT'S ALWAYS A LONE NUT—A WACKO!?"
...EVIDENCE SUBSTANTIATES THAT CHAPMAN DID NOT ACT ALONE...

MARK DAVID CHAPMAN—A PROBABLE C.I.A. MIND CONTROL SUBJECT PROGRAMMED WITH A COMBINATION OF HYPNOSIS & HYPNOTIC DRUGS ACTING UPON A PRIOR PREDISPOSED BELIEF PATTERN (IN AN ALREADY SUGGESTIBLE INDIVIDUAL) SIMILAR TO SIRHAN SIRHAN... AND MANY OTHERS!

A CHAPMAN PROGRAMMER-HYPNOTIST: DR. JULES BERNHARDT & C.I.A.!
C.I.A. SCIENTOLOGY CHURCH ALSO INVOLVED!

DON'T MOURN—ORGANIZE!

On the night of December 8, having finished a recording session, John Lennon and Yoko Ono returned to the Dakota Building, where Mark Chapman lay in wait with a revolver. Chapman fired five shots at close range, four of which hit Lennon. Although Lennon was rushed to hospital, staff could not revive him and he was pronounced dead soon after 11 P.M. The shooting caused a worldwide outpouring of grief.

1981

ABOVE: Ben Cross (far right) playing the role of Harold Abrahams in *Chariots of Fire*. The film, which was written by Colin Welland and directed by Hugh Hudson, was nominated for seven Academy Awards and won four, including Best Picture. It tells the true story of two athletes in the 1924 Olympics: Eric Liddell (Ian Charleson), a devout Scottish Christian who runs for the glory of God, and Abrahams, an English Jew who runs to overcome prejudice.

OPPOSITE: The first-ever London Marathon in 1981 saw 6,700 competitors running the 26 miles 385 yards from Greenwich Park to Buckingham Palace. Olympic runner Chris Brasher and fellow orienteer and Olympic steeplechaser John Disley initiated the London Marathon after Brasher had taken part in the New York Marathon and had been impressed by the spirit of the multi-ethnic event.

1981

LEFT AND OPPOSITE: The Prince and Princess of Wales leaving St. Paul's Cathedral and on the balcony of Buckingham Palace shortly after their wedding ceremony on July 29, 1981. Seven hundred million viewers across the world watched the fairy-tale marriage on television. Princess Diana would be the focus of world media for the next 16 years.

1981

LEFT AND OPPOSITE:
The eighties pendulum reaction to punk was the theatrical clothes, extravagant hairdos and makeup of the New Romantics. Bands such as Duran Duran, Spandau Ballet, Soft Cell, Human League, and Depeche Mode led the way on the music front. Boy George (left) formed Culture Club in 1981 and grew in popularity during the 1980s, but the band would break up in 1986 as a result of George's drug dependency.

1981

ABOVE: Aston Villa's Peter Withe fires a header into the back of the net in a game against Stoke City, helping to secure his team's position as the number one club in England after the 1980–81 season. Villa went on to win the 1982 European Cup, defeating Germany's Bayern Munich in the final.

OPPOSITE: Dee Hepburn and John Gordon Sinclair in the film *Gregory's Girl*. Written and directed by Bill Forsyth, the picture was a major hit and won Best Screenplay in that year's BAFTA Awards.

Herschel Walker of the University of Georgia Bulldogs goes over the top for a touchdown during a game against the University of Tennessee Volunteers on September 5, 1981, in Athens, Georgia. Walker, an All-American and Heisman Trophy winner while playing college football, went on to be a high-earning talent, first in the newly formed but short-lived United States Football League in 1983, then in the NFL, playing for the Dallas Cowboys, Minnesota Vikings, Philadelphia Eagles, and New York Giants.

1981

THE
COUNTY HALL

ABOVE: The funeral procession of Egyptian President Anwar Sadat moves through the streets of Cairo after he was assassinated by Islamic fundamentalists due in part to his peace treaty with Israel which outraged the Arab world. Vice-President Hosni Mubarak assumed control of the country upon Sadat's death.

OPPOSITE: Ken Livingstone, leader of the Greater London Council, is not fazed by protesters at his County Hall HQ in July 1981. Livingstone's left-wing policies earned him the nickname "Red Ken." He expressed sympathy with the plight of the Irish and in 1982 invited leaders of Sinn Féin to London. Protesters here are demonstrating for the release of IRA prisoners on hunger strike at the Maze Prison, Belfast, and demanding prisoner of war status for IRA prisoners within all Ulster jails.

1981

RIGHT: Denis Healey works on his speech for the Labour Party Conference on the beach at Brighton. Healey became deputy leader the previous year and was challenged for the deputy leadership at the Brighton conference by Tony Benn, giving the party the opportunity to test their new electoral college system. Healey retained his post wth a majority vote of less than 1 percent.

OPPOSITE: David Owen, William Rodgers, Shirley Williams, and Roy Jenkins were thrown out of the Labour Party for forming a Council for Social Democracy and later formed the Social Democratic Party. The "Gang of Four," as they became known, criticized Labour for drifting toward extremism and called for a classless struggle for social justice.

1981

The space shuttle program began life in the early 1970s as a cost-effective method to get astronauts and materials into orbit around the Earth. The first non-orbital flight took place in 1977 when the test craft *Enterprise* was launched from its 747 carrier. Dryden Flight Research Center at Edwards, California, seen in this photograph, was the hub of the program; although space mission launches took place from the Kennedy Space Center in Florida, return landings were usually at Edwards Air Force Base. The shuttle and its carrier are an iconic image of flight in the 1980s; in this photograph the massive rear engine cluster is covered by an aerodynamic cone during testing.

1981

On April 12, 1981, NASA launched the space shuttle *Columbia*. After orbiting the Earth 36 times, the shuttle returned two days later, landing at Edwards Air Force Base in California. Pictured here in November 1981, *Columbia* is in descent from its second space mission, which had to be cut short because of a fuel cell problem. During the flight the robot arm for deploying its payload was successfully tested and would be a crucial development for future missions.

1981

LEFT: In one of the most amazing comebacks in Test history, England recovered from a near innings defeat to beat Australia by 18 runs. Ian Botham (left) scored 149 to give England a chance and, with Australia still only needing 130 runs to win, Bob Willis took 8 wickets for 43 runs to secure victory.

OPPOSITE: Australia's Allan Border hits a six during the 1981 Ashes Series. England went on to take the Ashes, winning three Tests to Australia's one.

ABOVE: Tottenham Hotspur clinch the 1982 FA Cup after defeating Manchester City 3—2 in the final at Wembley. Here Ricky Villa scores the winning goal for Spurs.

OPPOSITE: Andrew Lloyd Webber (right), rock opera composer, pictured with cello virtuoso brother Julian. Andrew puts the finishing touches to his new musical *Cats*, based on T. S. Eliot's poetry, whose West End premiere took place at the New London Theatre in May 1981 and ran for a record-breaking 21 years. The Broadway production started a year later at the Winter Garden Theater and ran for 18 years—a Broadway record which would be broken by another Lloyd Webber production—*The Phantom of the Opera*.

LEFT: British band Bucks Fizz won the 1981 Eurovision Song Contest with catchy pop tune "Making Your Mind Up." Eurovision is an annual singing competition between the member states of the European Broadcasting Union.

OPPOSITE: The critically acclaimed police drama, *Hill Street Blues* started the first of seven seasons, winning eight Emmy awards in its debut year. The series marked a new sophistication in police drama, with separate storylines in different timeframes—sometimes extending over more than one episode. Focus on the tough conditions of urban living in the early 1980s emphasized the personal element of the characters, while handheld camera footage and other production devices gave a documentary feel to the show. *Hill Street Blues* was a turning point whose continuing influence may be seen in more recent police dramas, including *NYPD Blue* and *Homicide*.

1981

ABOVE: *Gallipoli*, the 1981 feature film Starring Mel Gibson and Mark Lee, is based on the notorious World War I campaign in the Dardanelles, Turkey. Directed by Australian Peter Weir, the picture gave Gibson his first serious movie role, though his international screen debut was maverick fantasy character Mad Max. The government-backed Australian New Wave cinema led to a resurgence, with 400 Australian films made between 1970 and 1985, often with an Australian historical or cultural theme.

OPPOSITE: A costumed participant sucks on an ice during the annual parade at Notting Hill Carnival, London. The summer festival originated in 1959 and by the 1980s had over 150,000 people attending. Early years were fraught as the Carnival took place without formal permission and police wanted to ban it. Growing larger, the Carnival developed a distinct African-Caribbean flavor which led to a period of racial tension. However, today it is one of London's best-loved events.

RIGHT: Tennis star Chris Evert Lloyd consoles husband John Lloyd. Evert won the Wimbledon Ladies' Singles for the third and final time in 1981 while John was knocked out in the second round. John Lloyd did better in mixed doubles, winning the Wimbledon title with Australian Wendy Turnbull in 1983 and 1984. The couple divorced in 1987.

OPPOSITE: Chris Evert receives the 1981 Ladies' Singles trophy from the Duchess of Kent on Centre Court at Wimbledon. She defeated Hana Mandlíková in straight sets.

1981

ABOVE: In 1981 legendary reggae star Bob Marley died from cancer at the age of 36. Marley left his homeland, Jamaica, in 1976 after an assassination attempt. During his self-imposed exile to Britain Marley recorded his *Exodus* album, which stayed in the British charts for 56 consecutive weeks. Marley went on to record the albums *Kaya* and *Survival*, releasing his final studio album, *Uprising*, in 1980.

OPPOSITE: Police with dogs round up skinheads after 400 of them went on a rampage in Southend-on-Sea, near London.

1981

LEFT: First Lady Nancy Reagan brought some style and glamour back to the White House following her husband's inauguration in January 1981. She also used her influence to pioneer the "Just Say No" campaign to stamp out recreational drug use across America.

OPPOSITE: Prince Charles pays a courtesy call to President Reagan at the White House during a visit to the USA in May 1981.

1981

RIGHT: Candlestick Park, January 10, 1982, in San Francisco, California. Everson Walls of the Dallas Cowboys is caught out of position as Dwight Clark of the San Francisco 49ers leaps to receive a six-yard catch off quarterback Joe Montana's pass in the end zone with 51 seconds left, lifting the 49er, past the Cowboys 28–27 in the 1981 NFC Championship Game and sending the 49ers to their first Super Bowl. Clark's grab is one of most famous catches in the history of the NFL and will forever be known as "The Catch."

OPPOSITE: *Coronation Street*, the soap opera set in the north of England, celebrated its 21st anniversary in 1981. Millions of viewers tuned in to watch the wedding of Ken and Deirdre Barlow, timed to coincide with the royal wedding of Prince Charles and Lady Diana Spencer in the summer of that year.

1981

LEFT: Space Invaders ushered in the modern craze for arcade games and made millions for its Japanese producer Taito. The two-dimensional game required the player to destroy as many alien vessels as possible before they could complete their invasion. With developments in technology, the arcade game would migrate to personal consoles and PCs to make video games one of the world's biggest media industries.

OPPOSITE: Even chimpanzees joined in with the 1980s craze for solving the Rubik's Cube. The three-dimensional puzzle, created by Hungarian architect Erno Rubik, became a global phenomenon and an icon of the eighties.

1981

RIGHT: Sir Freddie Laker displays the new air fares on flights to New York and Miami on his Skytrain service. Laker was ahead of his time in offering no-frills transatlantic fares. Laker Airways was initially a profitably run charter company but Laker spotted a gap in the market dominated by major airlines. The failure of the airline in 1982 was a combination of factors but especially the anti-competitive stance of the big operators. Virgin Atlantic would learn strategic lessons from Laker Skytrain when faced with similar aggression from British Airways.

OPPOSITE: Burnt-out cars and debris line the streets of Brixton following race riots in the South London neighborhood. Police had begun clamping down on street crime in the weeks leading up to the riots, and black men felt themselves unfairly targeted. With tensions running high, violent riots began when a crowd of residents believed the police to be arresting a black youth who had just been stabbed.

1981

OPPOSITE: Riots broke out in Northern Ireland following the death of Irish Republican Bobby Sands. He and other IRA inmates of the Maze Prison in Belfast had been on hunger strike, demanding to be treated as political prisoners rather than criminals. The British government refused to concede to their demands, despite Sands being elected as an MP to the British Parliament while incarcerated. Nine more inmates would die from their protest before the hunger strike ended in October.

ABOVE: More than 100,000 people lined the route of Bobby Sands' funeral procession in Belfast.

1981

ABOVE: President Reagan was shot by John Hinckley, Jr., as he left a speaking engagement at the Washington, DC, Hilton. Reagan's press secretary James Brady, policeman Thomas Delahanty, and Secret Service agent Timothy McCarthy were also wounded by the six shots fired in quick succession. The bullet that hit the President had ricocheted and lodged in his lung close to his heart. If all had gone to plan, each shot would have killed its intended victim as Hinckley had loaded bullets that explode on impact; fortunately they failed to detonate. Hinckley was ruled insane at his trial when it was discovered that his plan to kill the President was fueled by an obsession with actress Jodie Foster after seeing her in the movie *Taxi Driver*, whose protagonist, played by Robert De Niro, Hinckley used as a model.

OPPOSITE: US President Ronald Reagan moments before the assassination attempt which took place just 69 days into his presidency.

ABOVE: A curious student at a US computer camp looks inside the box. Apple led the consumer market by aggressively marketing their Apple II series to the education sector from 1977 Computer camps, with the intention of familiarizing young users with the fast developing digital world, began in the 1970s. In the heady days of the early 1980s high-end machines might boast 64 kilobytes of RAM!

OPPOSITE: An American surplus store demonstrates the ease with which guns could be bought and sold in the US. However, after the murder of John Lennon and the assassination attempt on President Reagan, anti-gun feeling increased, leading to growth in lobbying organizations such as Handgun Control, Inc. James Brady, paralysed in the Reagan shooting, added his voice to the call for increased legislation. However, the issue was hotly contested by the National Rifle Association, who claimed the Second Amendment right to possess and bear arms as a citizen's fundamental constitutional right.

1982

Guests leave the funeral of Princess Grace of Monaco, after she died aged 52, when her car left a winding mountain road and plummeted 120 feet. Princess Grace was pulled from the wreckage alive, only to die the next day from her injuries. Her daughter Princess Stephanie was alongside her and survived with spinal injuries. Princess Grace gave up her Hollywood career when she married Prince Rainer III in 1956; her last film, *High Society*, was made in the same year as her wedding. Ironically, among the world leaders present at her funeral was Princess Diana, who represented the Queen.

1982

LEFT: The BBC's popular Saturday morning children's show *Multi-Coloured Swap Shop* came to an end in 1982. Running for nearly 150 episodes, the program was broadcast live and engaged directly with its family audience by using the phone-in. Presenters Noel Edmunds, John Craven, Maggie Philbin, and Keith Chegwin, photographed here in their guise as rock band Brown Sauce, decided to seek out new challenges, none of which would be as rock musicians!

OPPOSITE: In 1982 folk duo Simon and Garfunkel embarked on a world tour following the success of their reunion concert in New York City's Central Park in 1981. The free concert was attended by 500,000 people and led to the release of live album *The Concert in Central Park* in 1982.

1982

OPPOSITE: The family sci-fi movie *E.T.: The Exra-Terrestrial* brought unique magic to the cinema when it was released in 1982. After his success with *Close Encounters of the Third Kind*, director Steven Spielberg was ready to return to the slightly scary theme of alien visitation, but this time for children. Spielberg drew on his vivid childhood imagination to create the story and the Extra-Terrestrial character at the heart of it. While capturing the sentiment familiar to Disney audiences, Spielberg was also innovative, including frightening scenes and creating an ugly central character to whom he gave big soulful eyes. Spielberg's smart marketing hook "ET Phone Home" was the equivalent of the alien call sign tune from *Close Encounters* and became a catchphrase around the world.

RIGHT: *E.T.*, like *Star Wars* before it, introduced a licensing opportunity for everything from T-shirts to bicycles and video games.

ABOVE: Swedish pop music phenomenon ABBA reached their 10th anniversary in 1982 and released their last studio album, *The Visitors*, and a compilation album, *The Singles: The First Ten Years*, in November 1982. At the end of 1982, the band went their separate ways, with Frida and Agnetha going solo and Bjorn and Benny still working in partnership on a number of projects including collaboration with Tim Rice on the musical *Chess*.

OPPOSITE: Pete Townshend of The Who in concert in Birmingham during the band's farewell tour in September 1982; the tour was a sell-out in the USA and the highest grossing of the year. After the death of Keith Moon in 1978, Kenny Jones, the former Faces drummer, had been drafted in and the band went on to release two further studio albums, *Face Dances* in 1981 and *It's Hard* in 1982.

1982

RIGHT: *Actor* Christopher Reeve, accompanied here by his English girlfriend Gae Exton, is en route to Calgary to film *Superman III*. At this point in his career Reeve was balancing his Hollywood roles, which commanded a minimum fee of $1m, with theater work, his first love. His commitment to acting included transforming his physique for the role of Superman, putting on 30 pounds of muscle with a training regime supervised by former weight lifter David Prowse, who played Darth Vader in *Star Wars*.

OPPOSITE: In the cult sci-fi movie *Blade Runner*, directed by Ridley Scott, Harrison Ford plays Deckard, tasked with tracking down renegade "replicants" played by Daryl Hannah and Rutger Hauer. Here, Joanna Cassidy plays a dangerous replicant masquerading as a snake dancer. The film's complex story line was derived from Philip K. Dick's novel, *Do Androids Dream of Electric Sheep?*, and was made into a gothic masterpiece by Scott's cinematography, oppressive sets, and atmospheric lighting.

1982

ABOVE: Olympic swimmer Sharron Davies takes a break from the pool to swim with dolphins. Davies, who won silver in the 400 meters medley at the 1980 Moscow Olympic Games, decided at the age of 18 to make a career change, moving into modeling and developing her media profile. Davies continues to be a high-profile spokesperson and commentator in the world of sport.

OPPOSITE: Leader of the Opposition, Labour MP Michael Foot walks Dizzy the dog in his hometown of Tredegar, South Wales. Foot, who became an MP during the 1945 general election, led the Labour Party to lose the 1983 election to Margaret Thatcher. The relatively left-wing manifesto was blamed for the defeat and Foot resigned the leadership to make way for Neil Kinnock.

1982

LEFT: After a very public pregnancy, the Princess of Wales gave birth to a son on June 21, 1982, at St. Mary's Hospital in Paddington, London. It was his parents' wish that he was born in hospital rather than in Buckingham Palace. It was another seven days before his name was officially announced as William Arthur Philip Louis.

OPPOSITE: An official photograph shows the Queen, the Queen Mother, and Prince Philip with the Prince and Princess of Wales and the baby prince, who was now second in line to the throne.

ABOVE: At a critical point in the Iran–Iraq War, victorious Iranian soldiers crowd in for a photograph following the liberation of Ahvaz, the provincial capital of Khuzestan, in May 1982. Iraq captured this strategically important area early in the war and made a strong defence against the Iranian attack. To Iraq's surprise Iran's military determination withstood their counter-attack. But the conflict would rage on with trench warfare reminiscent of World War I for another six years.

OPPOSITE: PLO Leader Yasser Arafat inspects the bomb damage in Beirut following an Israeli attack in August 1982. Lebanon became the involuntary epicenter of the Middle East conflict from the mid 1970s. In addition to an internal political divide, the settlement of 300,000 Palestinian refugees in camps throughout Lebanon created a humanitarian disaster and a military threat to Lebanon itself and neighboring Israel. In June Israel invaded southern Lebanon and swiftly approached Beirut, which it shelled for 10 weeks. The intention was to remove Palestinian combatants from southern Lebanon where they threatened Israel's border, but the Israeli action had many bloody consequences.

1982

OPPOSITE AND ABOVE: In 1982 Queen released the funk album *Hot Space* which was a change of direction toward dance music, based on the success of their single "Another One Bites the Dust." Included on the album was "Under Pressure," a collaboration with David Bowie that topped the charts in Europe in 1981. The band toured to promote the new album in Europe, Japan, and North America but would not tour again in North America until 2006 with a new lineup, after Freddie Mercury's death. In 1982 Queen left Elektra Records, their label in the United States, Canada, Japan, Australia, and New Zealand, signing with EMI/Capitol Records.

ABOVE: Pope John Paul II attends a youth festival at Edinburgh's Murrayfield stadium in May 1982. Forty thousand young Scots crammed into the stadium in the hope of seeing the Pontiff on the first ever visit of a Pope to Britain. During his six day visit he traveled to Wales as well as Scotland and also visited Buckingham Palace for a private meeting with the Queen.

OPPOSITE: *Fort Apache the Bronx*, the police drama movie starred Paul Newman and was a box office success, touching on unsettling social issues summed up in the title, which implies that the 41st Precinct station in the decayed slum area of the South Bronx was like a

1982

OPPOSITE: Following on from their successful US tour in 1981, the Rolling Stones toured Europe in 1982. Here Mick Jagger, Keith Richards and Ronnie Wood strut their stuff. The tour promoted their 1981 album *Tattoo You* and took in 36 shows.

RIGHT: Sting began pursuing solo projects in the early 1980s, starring in the film of Dennis Potter's *Treacle and Brimstone* in 1982. That same year he began dating actress Trudie Styler as his marriage to Frances Tomelty broke down.

1982

LEFT: Survivors are helped onshore at Bluff Cove, East Falklands, after two British troop carrying vessels, *Sir Galahad* and *Sir Tristram*, were bombed by Argentine airforce attacks while the boats were unloading troops. One week later the Argentine forces surrendered Port Stanley, ending the 74 days of conflict in the Falklands War during which 258 Britons and 649 Argentines died.

OPPOSITE: HMS *Hermes*, flagship of the British Falklands Task Force, returns to a flotilla welcome in Portsmouth, England, on July 21. Prime Minister Margaret Thatcher was taken on board prior to docking and spent over an hour talking with officers and carrying out an inspection of the ship's company.

1982

OPPOSITE: British Prime Minister Margaret Thatcher interrupts reporters' questions to hurry President Reagan on his way after the pair met for a working breakfast at Downing Street. The two leaders became renowned for their close relationship based on similar conservative views on government and economics.

ABOVE: President Reagan with the Queen at a royal banquet at Windsor Castle.

1983

Fans of top British band Duran Duran show their appreciation of lead singer Simon le Bon's performance. The band comprised five members who shared the same ideas about visual impact, dressing themselves with careful style, and using the recent music video medium to brilliant effect. They enlisted the skills of film directors Godley and Creme, former members of rock band 10cc, to make the most controversial video of the time to accompany their single "Girls on Film." The video was banned by the BBC—a move guaranteed to increase the success of anything at that time. Popularity with MTV assured the band a strong following in the USA and 1983 was likened to a smaller-scale repeat of Beatlemania.

ABOVE: Emerging from the New Romantic movement, Spandau Ballet released their second studio album, *Diamond,* in 1982. The clean good looks of the band and the strong vocals of lead singer Tony Hadley gave them a distinctive look and sound and a big fanbase. Here a tartan clad fan is warmly sandwiched between band members Martin and Gary Kemp.

OPPOSITE: A big scream from pop singer Toyah Wilcox. In 1981 she hit the charts with "It's a Mystery" and "I Want to Be Free" and was voted Best Female Singer at the British Rock and Pop Awards in 1982. Toyah married guitarist Robert Fripp in 1986.

1983

RIGHT: Gdansk shipyard worker Lech Walesa, the founder of the independent trade union movement Solidarity, arrives at Heathrow Airport following his release from prison in his native Poland. He was arrested in 1981 when the Polish authorities declared martial law and clamped down upon dissenting political movements. Two years later, in 1983, he won the Nobel Peace Prize. After the Polish constitution was amended in 1990 to allow freer elections he won a landslide victory and was President of Poland for five years.

OPPOSITE: In April 1983 Campaign for Nuclear Disarmament (CND) supporters formed a human chain that linked Burghfield (location of a nuclear weapons factory), Aldermaston (home of Britain's Atomic Weapons Research Establishment), and Greenham Common (a British air force base for nuclear armaments). The protest was peaceful and no arrests were made. A "peace camp" was maintained at Greenham Common from 1981 until 2000.

ABOVE: TV-AM began broadcasting on ITV in the UK in February 1983. The breakfast television show had a host of heavyweight presenters: (from left to right) Robert Kee, Angela Rippon, David Frost, Anna Ford, and Michael Parkinson, but they failed to win the ratings war with rival BBC show *Breakfast Time* and most of these presenters found themselves axed within months.

OPPOSITE: *Top of the Pops* presents Top of the DJs: lined up here in May 1983 are the long-running TV chart show's presenters during a celebration of its 1,000th edition. Ed Stewpot Stewart pours champagne into Janice Long's glass while Jimmy Savile enjoys taking center stage.

1983

OPPOSITE: Vice-President George Bush meets Prime Minister Margaret Thatcher at Downing Street, flanked by members of the secret service. Former CIA Director Bush ran for the presidency in the 1980 elections. Beaten by Reagan, Bush was selected as Vice-President by Reagan and he remained in that office until becoming the 41st President of the United States in 1989. In 1983 both Thatcher and Reagan had their eye on the electorate, with UK elections in 1983 and US elections looming in 1984.

LEFT: Prolific Soviet writer and dissident Alexandr Solzenhitzyn received the Templeton Prize in 1983.

1983

ABOVE: The five Doctors appear together in a feature length edition to celebrate 20 years of *Dr. Who*, which to date is the longest-running TV sci-fi show, with over 700 episodes broadcast since 1963. *Dr. Who* achieved international success with the series broadcast on PBS in the USA. The publicity photoshoot had to improvise missing Doctors with stand-ins (l-r) a wax model of Tom Baker, Peter Davidson, Jon Pertwee, Patrick Troughton and Richard Hurndall (look-alike of the late William Hartnell, the original Doctor).

OPPOSITE: Demonstrators chant, "Reagan-Thatcher hands off Grenada" as they protest the US invasion of Grenada, a former British colony which was ruled by a left-wing government that had seized power in 1979. When the incumbent Prime Minister of Grenada, Maurice Bishop, was executed in 1983 President Reagan feared the "Cuban workers" would exert more influence in the island, making it another base for Soviet Communism in the Carribean. The US invasion successfully changed the regime but it was one of the few low points in the Anglo American special relationship during the Reagan-Thatcher years.

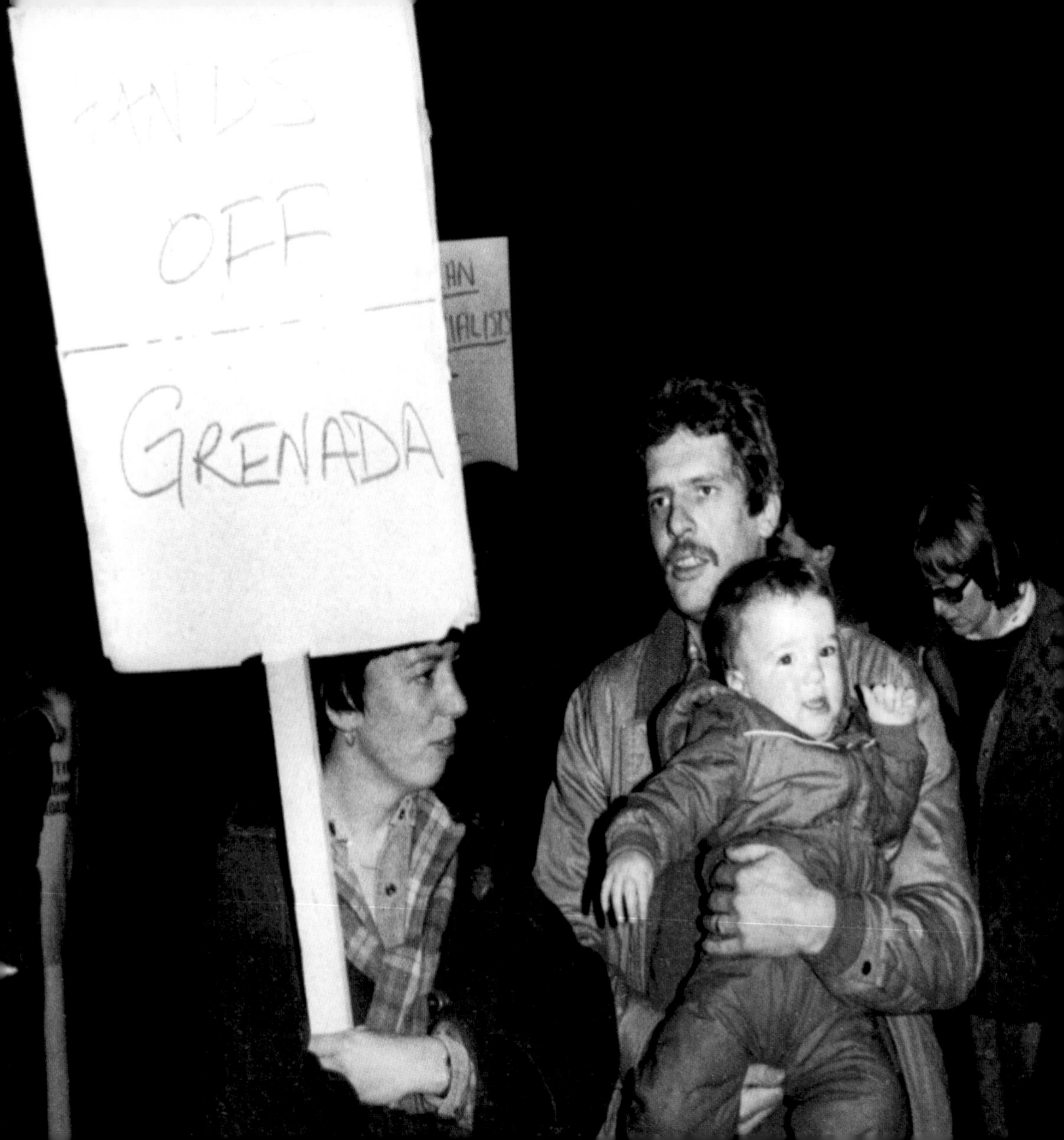
OFF
GRENADA

1983

LEFT: Sigourney Weaver and Mel Gibson on the set of Peter Weir's political thriller *The Year of Living Dangerously* which was shown at the Cannes Festival in 1983. Based on a novel by C. J. Koch set in Jakarta, the story follows two journalists caught up in a violent attempted coup in 1965. Weir had the backing of MGM for the movie, which enabled him to match *Gallipoli* star Gibson with an internationally renowned cast. The movie received good reviews in America and won an Oscar for actress Linda Hunt.

OPPOSITE: Brazilian racing driver Ayrton Senna's team pack away his Rait-Toyota car. Senna's climb to the top of world motorsport continued with a hard-won victory over Martin Brundle in the 1983 Marlboro British Formula Three Championship. Senna would make his Formula One debut in 1984, driving for Ted Toleman's team.

1983

ABOVE: On October 23, 1983, the US Marine Barracks at Beirut Airport were hit with a massive suicide bomb hidden in a truck. Here rescue workers search the wreckage for survivors. Two hundred and forty-one US military personnel lost their lives in the bombing, 220 of them Marines. Minutes later, a French paratroop unit suffered a similar attack in West Beirut, killing 58 French troops. Responsibility for the attacks was claimed by Islamic Jihad but ultimately it was believed to be the action of Iran-backed Hezbollah groups.

OPPOSITE: A US marine stands in front of the ruins of the US Marine Barracks in Beirut, Lebanon, the day after it was bombed. The terrorist action had the desired effect of forcing the withdrawal of the UN Peacekeeping Force in Lebanon, of which both the Marines and the French paratroops formed part.

1984

OPPOSITE: Magic Johnson (right) of the Los Angeles Lakers battles for position against Larry Bird of the Boston Celtics during a game at the Great Western Forum in Inglewood, California, in 1984. Both players entered the NBA the same year—1979—from the college draft and took their respective teams into a showstopping rivalry for the NBA Championship throughout the 1980s. Although portrayed as arch-enemies in a famous 1986 Converse commercial, the players were good friends off court.

LEFT: Ice skating duo Torvill and Dean won gold for Britain in ice dancing at the Winter Olympics in Sarajevo in 1984. They wowed the judges with a flawless performance set to "Boléro" by Maurice Ravel and were the only pair to score top marks from every judge.

1984

OPPOSITE: Jerry Hall and Mick Jagger pictured in July 1984. Six-foot-tall Texan Hall, first met Jagger in New York in 1977 while she was a top-earning model and engaged to Roxy Music frontman Bryan Ferry. In March 1984 Hall gave birth to the first of the couple's four children, Elizabeth Scarlett. Jagger and Hall would not marry until 1990, divorcing nine years later.

RIGHT: Singer Rod Stewart en route from Spain to Los Angeles without his new girlfriend Kelly Emberg. Stewart released "Infatuation," "Some Guys Have All the Luck," and "All Right Now" in the same year.

1984

LEFT AND OPPOSITE: Prime Minister Margaret Thatcher dances at a reception with Brighton's mayor John Blackman during the Conservative Party annual conference in Brighton. Just a few hours later, at 2:45 A.M. on October 12, a powerful IRA bomb destroyed part of the Grand Hotel where Thatcher and members of her cabinet were staying. The Prime Minister narrowly escaped death but five people lost their lives, including MP Sir Anthony Berry and Roberta Wakeham, wife of Parliamentary Secretary to the Treasury John Wakeham. IRA member Patrick Magee, who received eight life sentences for planting the bomb, cited Thatcher's stance on Bobby Sands and the Maze hunger-strikers as the justification for the attack. Magee was released in 1999 under the terms of the Good Friday agreement.

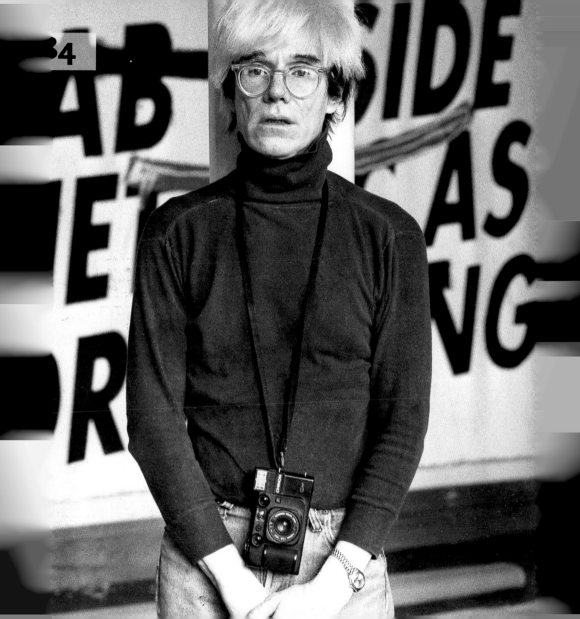

RIGHT: Cover model Brooke Shields began her career while a baby and continued as a popular teen model. In 1978, aged 11, she filmed *Pretty Baby* and in 1980 appeared in *The Blue Lagoon*. From 1983 to 1987 Brooke took time out from her acting career to study French literature at Princeton, but managed to find time for a cameo in the 1984 Muppet adventure, *The Muppets Take Manhattan*.

OPPOSITE: Andy Warhol poses for a photograph in 1984. Warhol rose to fame in the 1960s as a leading exponent of Pop Art. He experienced a resurgence in the early 1980s, socializing with rock stars such as Mick Jagger and Debbie Harry, becoming much in demand as an album cover designer. Warhol made two cable television series, *Andy Warhol's TV* and *Andy Warhol's Fifteen Minutes,* for MTV prior to his death in 1987 following gall bladder surgery.

ABOVE AND OPPOSITE: The 1980s saw the street culture art of breakdancing spreading from New York to the rest of the world. The international craze, which incorporated elements of acrobatics, gymnastics, mime, and martial arts, was popularized by movies such as the musical *Flashdance* and the more dramatic hip-hop feature film *Beat Street* in 1984. Accompanying the breakdance craze came the "boombox" or "ghetto blaster," used to play custom-made samples and music mixes at high volume.

1984

ABOVE: Dan Aykroyd (left), Bill Murray (center), and Harold Ramis star in the 1984 science fiction comedy *Ghostbusters*. The movie was written by co-stars Aykroyd and Ramis and also starred Sigourney Weaver, for whom the comic role was a new departure. The 1989 sequel, *Ghostusters II: River of Slime*, achieved what was at the time the biggest three-day opening weekend gross earnings in history, a record that was broken just one week later by *Batman*.

OPPOSITE: *The Right Stuff* was a film adaptation of the novel by Tom Wolfe. The epic movie traces the history of the test pilots who were involved in high-speed aeronautical research at Edwards Air Force Base, leading to the selection of astronauts for Project Mercury, the United States' first attempt at manned spaceflight. At the Academy Awards ceremony in 1984 the film won four out of its eight nominations.

1984

LEFT AND OPPOSITE: A policewoman lays flowers at the site where colleague Yvonne Fletcher was gunned down while policing a protest outside the Libyan Embassy in London. Fletcher was killed when someone inside the Embassy opened fire. The police laid siege to the building for 11 days, prompting the Libyan leader Colonel Gaddafi to order a siege of the British Embassy in Tripoli. Eventually the British government allowed the Libyan Embassy staff to leave the building (opposite) to return home and promptly broke off diplomatic relations with Gaddafi's government.

1984

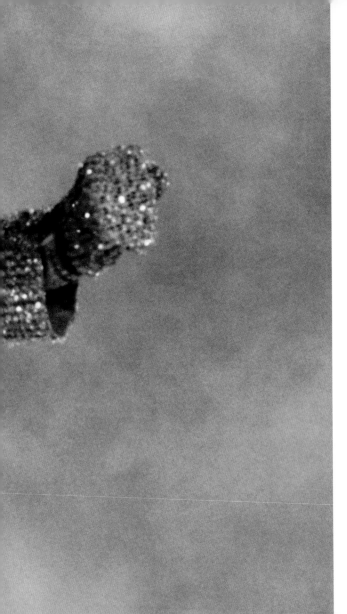

1984 was another eventful year for Michael Jackson. Here he is pictured in concert in Buffalo, New York, in 1984. Jackson was enjoying the success of his 1982 solo album *Thriller*, but was still working with his brothers in the Jackson Five. *Thriller* did not have an official tour to promote it, but the 1984 Victory Tour, to promote the Jacksons' *Victory* album, included much of Michael's solo material.

In 1984 Jackson was honored at the Grammy Awards when he received 12 nominations and scooped eight out of his lifetime total of 13 Grammys. He was also invited to the White House to receive an award from President Ronald Reagan for his support of charities that helped people overcome alcohol and drug abuse.

However, there was also a major setback at the beginning of the year when Michael and other members of the Jacksons filmed a commercial for Pepsi Cola; in front of a full house of fans during a simulated concert, pyrotechnics accidentally set his hair on fire and he suffered second-degree burns to his scalp.

1984

ABOVE: Richard Branson celebrates the maiden voyage of his new airline, Virgin Atlantic, in June 1984. Initially flights ran between London Gatwick and New York Newark, with a single aircraft—a leased Boeing 747-200—but Virgin has since expanded its fleet and the number of routes, carrying over 65 million passengers to date.

OPPOSITE: Boy George of Culture Club returns to England following a trip to the United States. The band's latest hit, "Karma Chameleon," spent three weeks at the top of the *Billboard* Top 100 in 1984 and Culture Club was awarded a Grammy the same year.

1984

LEFT: Czechoslovakian Ivan Lendl won the French Open in 1984, defeating John McEnroe in a dramatic five set final. A year earlier, Lendl had irked the Czechoslovak government by participating in a tournament in South Africa, which was boycotted by many countries and sporting organizations because of its apartheid policies. His subsequent ostracism in Czechoslovakia led him to seek US citizenship.

OPPOSITE: Heavyweight boxer Frank Bruno gets a hug from his manager Terry Lawless after a four-and-a-half-minute KO of Canada's Ken Lakusta at Wembley, London. The relief was palpable since this victory was preceded by Bruno's knockout defeat by American James "Bonecrusher" Smith four months earlier.

1984

OPPOSITE: Gary Brabham (right) and Damon Hill, sons of illustrious racing-driver fathers, pose for the cameras. Despite his background, Hill found it difficult to get into motorsport and he made his start in motorcycle racing, which he funded himself. This later picture shows Hill now firmly on track, via Formula Ford and Formula Three, to being Formula One World Champion in 1996. By coincidence, Hill's first Formula One ticket was with Team Brabham. Gary Brabham was less successful and retired from racing in 1995.

RIGHT: Britain's Zola Budd, running without shoes, closes in on America's Mary Decker during the 3,000 meter final at the Los Angeles Olympics. The two women came into contact shortly after this picture was taken and race favorite Decker fell to the ground. Decker could not continue and Budd only managed seventh place amid the jeers of the predominantly American crowd.

ABOVE: Fitness was one of the great fads of the 80s. Here Angie Best, estranged wife of soccer star George, joined in as 774 women in leotards, and men in T-shirts and shorts, sweated their way through a rigorous routine in the bright sunshine.

OPPOSITE: Musician and entertainer Roy Castle shows off his Commodore 64 home computer. The keyboard and processor, disk drive, screen monitor, and ancillary equipment all stand on a trolley built by Castle himself. His state of the art computer could even be programmed to print out the famous Roy Castle trademark, seen here on the screen—a trumpet.

1984

RIGHT: In 1984 Mikhail Gorbachev became the first senior Soviet politician to visit London for almost three decades, signaling a thaw in East—West relations. Gorbachev, who was widely expected to become the next Soviet leader, made a positive impression on the "Iron Lady," Margaret Thatcher, who announced she had found a man "with whom she could do business."

OPPOSITE: Gorbachev's wife Raisa gets a taste of the West during her tour of Marks and Spencer's flagship store at Marble Arch in London.

1984

Ed Moses of the USA clears a hurdle en route to victory in the men's 400 meters hurdles final at the 1984 Olympic Games in Los Angeles, California. Moses's stamina, strength, and technique in the 400 meters hurdles was such that he dominated the event for almost a decade, with few challengers. Indeed, he achieved the longest winning streak in athletics, with 122 victories between losing to Harold Schmid in Berlin in August 1977 and then to Danny Harris in Madrid in June 1987. During this period of domination, the quality of hurdling improved enormously, but so did Moses. His Olympic career may have suffered a hiatus thanks to the US boycott of the 1980 Olympics in Moscow, when it was likely he would have repeated his 1976 gold-winning performance. In the 1988 Olympics he took the bronze medal; astonishingly, this was the first time he had been defeated in a championship event. Moses set his first world record in the event in 1976 at 47.63 seconds and lowered it to 47.02 seconds in several stages by 1983, where it stood until Kevin Young of the USA ran 46.79 seconds in the Olympic final of 1992.

1984

LEFT: Rock star Elton John as a pantomime dame during rehearsals for a charity performance of *Mother Goose* at the Theatre Royal, Drury Lane, London. In this one night only special he appeared alongside veteran actor Sir John Gielgud.

OPPOSITE: Yoko Ono and Sean Lennon visit Liverpool, the city of John's birth. 1984 marked Yoko's 50th birthday and for that event a tribute album, *Every Man Has a Woman*, an unfinished project of John Lennon's, was released in her honor, with stars such as Elvis Costello, Harry Nilsson, and Roberta Flack recording covers of Yoko's own songs.

ABOVE: Irish loyalist leader the Reverend Ian Paisley addresses a demonstration in London's Trafalgar Square. Paisley bitterly opposed the 1985 Anglo-Irish Treaty, which gave the Republic of Ireland a small role in the government of Northern Ireland in the hope of ending the Troubles.

OPPOSITE: Vice-President Bush holds a press conference en route to Moscow to represent the United States at the funeral of Soviet leader Yuri Andropov, whose successor was 72-year-old Konstantin Chernenko. It was apparent that these old men of the Revolution were ailing and Chernenko was visibly unwell at Andropov's funeral. Although Chernenko was appointed leader of the Soviet Union, by the end of the year it was clear his days were numbered.

1984

OPPOSITE: Welsh acting legend Richard Burton died of a cerebral hemorrhage at the young age of 58. Here his body is carried to its final resting place at a cemetery near his home in Celigny in Switzerland. The seven-times Oscar-nominated star was most famous for his two marriages to Elizabeth Taylor between 1964 and 1976.

ABOVE: British miners clash with police in London's Parliament Square during the miners' strike of 1984–5. Thousands of men walked out in the dispute over pit closures announced by the Thatcher government. The strike was one of the longest in British history and was marred by violence. The miners were eventually forced to return to work and the pit closures went ahead.

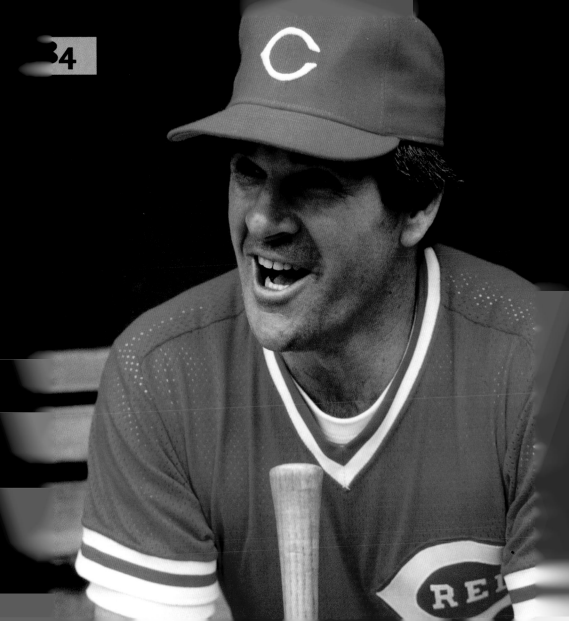

OPPOSITE: Pete Rose of the Cincinnati Reds during batting practice before a Major League Baseball game against the Chicago Cubs in September 1984. Legendary hitter Rose spent his best years with the Reds, joining them in 1963 then being briefly tempted away by the Phillies in 1979 with a record-breaking four-year contract. 1984 saw Rose back with the Reds in the role of player-manager. Already the second-ever member of the 4,000 hit club, in 1985 he took the hitting record from Ty Cobb when he made his 4,192nd hit, in a San Diego Padres game.

RIGHT: British Olympic gold medal decathlete Daley Thompson makes eye contact with arch rival, West German Juergen Hingsen, on the track. Thompson's performance in the decathlon during the late 1970s and the 1980s made it one of the most exciting events of the 1980 and 1984 Olympics, especially with such a close fought competition with Hingsen, who was taking records from Thompson as fast as Daley took them from him. But, unfortunately for Hingsen, Daley was usually the better athlete on the day. In 1984, Thompson repeated his 1980 gold medal performance, coolly whistling his way through "God Save the Queen" on the podium.

1984

American Carl Lewis accelerates down the runway of the long jump during the 1984 Summer Olympics in Los Angeles, California. By 1984, Carl Lewis was one of the biggest sporting celebrities in the world, top in sprinting and long jump, but owing to track and field's relatively low profile in America, Lewis was not nearly as well known there. The 1984 Olympic Games in Los Angeles made Lewis a household name after he came away with four gold medals.

1984

OPPOSITE AND RIGHT:
In 1984 severe drought compounded with civil war to cause a terrible famine in Ethiopia. The fighting hindered the relief of international aid and the Ethiopian government was widely condemned for disporportionate military spending and withholding aid from rebel-held territories. The victims of famine could not be catalogued with certainty, but hundreds of thousands died from starvation and disease while millions were made destitute, being forced away from their barren lands by drought or forced to flee from conflict zones.

1984

LEFT: Rock singer and organizer of Live Aid, Bob Geldof, outside SARM Studios in London during the recording of the British Live Aid single "Do They Know It's Christmas?" in November 1984. Geldof relentlessly promoted the single to make it a huge seasonal hit. The single was released in aid of Ethiopian famine relief and featured a range of famous artists including Duran Duran, George Michael, Bananarama, Sting, and Bono. Geldof persuaded Boy George to take a flying break from Culture Club's US tour, arriving by Concorde in time to record his solo piece. Geldof also shamed the British government into donating the VAT charged on the single to the Live Aid cause.

OPPOSITE: Bob Geldof was tireless in bringing the plight of starving people in East Africa to the attention of the world, but almost on a daily basis, photographs and news reports told their own story of suffering.

1984

ABOVE: Girl group Bananarama released a self-titled album in 1984, which included the songs "Cruel Summer" and "Robert De Niro's Waiting." "Cruel Summer" gained the British threesome some recognition in America, where it reached number nine in the *Billboard* Hot 100.

OPPOSITE: Tony Hadley and Martin Kemp of Spandau Ballet arrive to record their parts for a single for Band Aid. They were alongside a host of other pop stars who took part in Bob Geldof's Ethiopian appeal.

1984

OPPOSITE: Sting became a proud new father in January 1984 when his girlfriend Trudie Styler gave birth to a baby girl, Bridget Michael. Sting admitted he missed the actual birth, having popped out for a bite to eat.

LEFT: Paul and Linda McCartney arrive at Uxbridge Magistrates Court in West London, where Linda was fined for possession of a small amount of cannabis.

1984

LEFT: Riot police confront Liverpool fans during the 1984 European Cup final between Liverpool and Roma at the Olympic Stadium in Rome. Liverpool won the match 4–2 on penalties after their goalkeeper Bruce Grobbelaar famously distracted the Roma penalty takers by wobbling his legs.

OPPOSITE: Soviet Russian Troops entered Afghanistan in 1979 when invited by the Marxist government, who wanted their support against the Mujahideen who forcibly opposed the anti-Islamic reforms being imposed on Afghans by the government. During their 10-year occupation, more than 14,000 Russian soldiers died and nearly half a million were wounded or disabled by illness. This picture shows Russian soldiers captured by the Mujahideen.

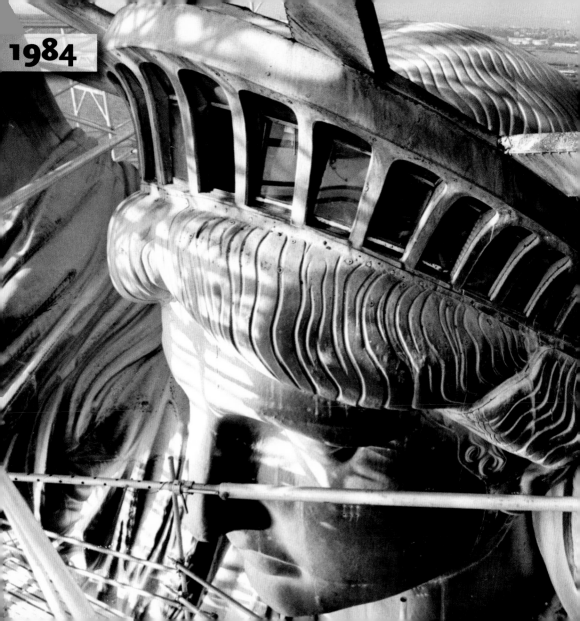
1984

OPPOSITE AND RIGHT:
Premier icon of New
York City and the USA,
the Statue of Liberty was
closed for two years in
1984 for a $62 million
renovation prior to the
statue's centennial in
1986. Constructed with a
copper skin over a steel
frame, the statue was
prefabricated by Gustave
Eiffel's engineering works
in France and arrived
in 350 pieces by boat in
1885; it was a gift from
the Republic of France
to the United States to
mark the first centenary
of the US Declaration of
Independence. Chrysler
chairman Lee Iacocca
was appointed by
President Reagan to head
the Statue of Liberty–Ellis
Island Foundation,
tasked with renovation
and preservation of these
two heritage sites. In
the background of the
photograph (right) the
Chrysler Building can just
be seen—an art deco
symbol of New York's
architectural heritage.

1985

ABOVE: The first episode of the award-winning *EastEnders* was broadcast on February 19, 1985. The long-running BBC soap opera focused on the everyday lives of the inhabitants of Albert Square in the fictitious Borough of Walford, East London. Much of the action centers around the Queen Victoria pub—commonly referred to as the Queen Vic. Here the cast is photographed on set at the BBC's Elstree studio.

OPPOSITE: Arnold Schwarzenegger publicizes his new movie *Conan the Destroyer*, the 1984 sequel to *Conan the Barbarian*—a big success in 1982. Although the Conan follow-up was a success, it was overshadowed by his other movie *The Terminator*, James Cameron's slick action sci-fi film, rapturously received by a cinema audience hungry for fast-paced fantasy. The cyborg assassin gave Arnie his signature role.

ABOVE: Police move in to quell riots in the Broadwater Farm housing estate in Tottenham, North London. The riots broke out after local resident Cynthia Jarrett died of a heart attack while police searched her home following the arrest of her son. The riots were notable for their extreme violence, with Police Constable Keith Blakelock being hacked to death.

OPPOSITE: Two victims blinded by the gas leak from the Union Carbide plant in Bhopal, India, stand outside the plant after the disaster. Two thousand people died in the immediate aftermath and as many as 200,000 more suffered long-term health problems, including blindness and liver and kidney failure.

1985

LEFT: Vincent Edward "Bo" Jackson poses in 1985, his final college season for Auburn, where he displayed talent in baseball, football, and on the track as a sprinter, winning the Heisman Trophy for his performance in the 1985 football season. He moved on to a professional career in both MLB and NFL. Tampa Bay Buccaneers selected him from the 1986 draft but he started out playing baseball for Kansas City Royals instead; in 1987 he signed with the LA Raiders football team, which allowed him to play part time during the baseball season, when he was also playing for the Royals.

OPPOSITE: Soccer stars Ian Rush and Kenny Dalglish in celebratory mood. Their partnership as strikers was the most prolific of the 1980s. After signing for Liverpool Football Club in 1980, Rush scored 229 goals in 469 appearances while "King Kenny" netted 118 times in 355 games.

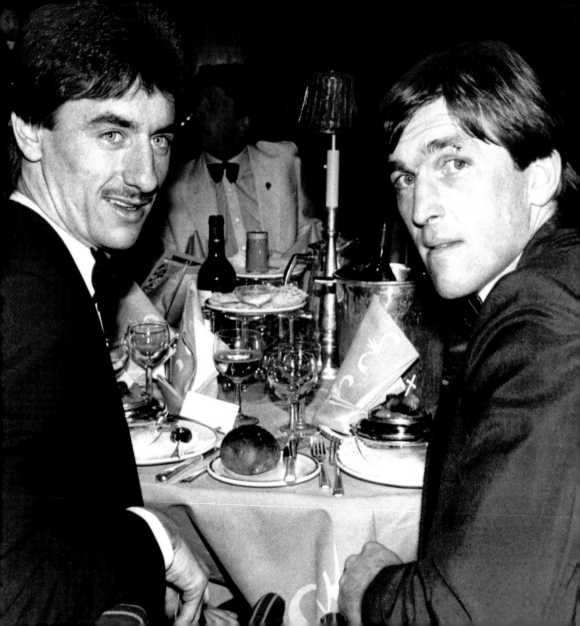

1985

LEFT AND OPPOSITE:
Mobile telephones were beginning to appear in the mid 1980s. The need for a large battery made the phones so big that they often came with a shoulder strap or were fitted in cars. They became a status symbol for the 1980s "yuppie"; hefty fees, expensive handsets, and limited network coverage meant that they had not yet achieved widespread popularity.

1985

RIGHT: Boy George quashes rumors that he plans to quit Britain ahead of touring France and Germany by wearing a Union Jack shirt and dyeing his hair red, white, and blue. Culture Club's record "The War Song" was number one across Europe at the time. Taken from their 1984 album *Waking Up with the House on Fire*, it was the only hit single from the album, which compared disappointingly with their previous *Colour By Numbers*. George was well on the way to a serious heroin addiction that would soon break up the band.

OPPOSITE: David Bowie performs at the Live Aid concert at Wembley Stadium, London, where the crowd went wild for his 29-minute set. Also for Live Aid, he and Mick Jagger collaborated on a cover of Martha & the Vandellas' hit "Dancing in the Street," which was screened on pre-recorded video directed by David Mallet in London's Dockland. The street party spirit reached its height when, at JFK Stadium, Philadelphia, during his duet with Tina Turner, Jagger tore off Turner's skirt so she could dance more freely.

1985

OPPOSITE AND ABOVE: Rock and pop stars come together for the Live Aid concerts in London and Philadelphia on July 13, 1985. The concerts, which were the brainchild of former Boomtown Rats band member Bob Geldof, followed on from the success of the 1984 Band Aid single "Do They Know It's Christmas?" which raised millions for famine victims in Africa. Having visited Ethiopia to oversee the distribution of aid from the money raised, Geldof realized the need for a more organized approach to tackling the immense problems and the Live Aid project was conceived.

1985

The American segment of the multi-venue rock concert was held in front of an estimated audience of 99,000 at the JFK Stadium in Philadelphia. Bob Dylan, Led Zeppelin, Tina Turner, Madonna, and Rolling Stones frontman Mick Jagger were just a few famous names who performed to help raise funds for famine relief. Many other countries including Australia, the Netherlands, Russia, and Germany were inspired by Live Aid and held their own concerts.

1985

Described as "The Day
Rock and Roll Changed
the World," the Live
Aid concerts featured
16 hours of live music
and were watched by
over 1.5 billion people
worldwide. The London
concert closed with the
anthem "Do They Know
It's Christmas?", which
was the inspiration for
Geldof's ambitious
plan, while the US finale
was the rousing USA
for Africa's "We Are
the World." Seen on
stage here are Lionel
Ritchie, Dionne Warwick,
Peter, Paul, and Mary,
Bob Dylan, and Harry
Belafonte. During the
finale, Bob Dylan broke
a string on his guitar so
Rolling Stone Ronnie
Wood handed over his
guitar to Dylan and
played air guitar until a
technician came onstage
with a replacement.

1985

ABOVE: Bruce Springsteen on stage with Nils Lofgren, a member of his E Street Band, during the Born in the USA Tour. "The Boss" released the *Born in the USA* album in June 1984 before embarking on a tour of Europe, Asia, and North America between July 1984 and October 1985.

OPPOSITE: Ringo Starr and his wife Barbara Bach (center) joined Olivia Harrison, wife of George, at a fashion show in 1985. Earlier in the year Ringo became the first Beatle to be a grandfather after his son Zak had a daughter, Tatia Jayne.

OPPOSITE: Fifty-four people lost their lives when the engine of their Boeing 737 caught fire during takeoff at Manchester Airport. The flight was packed as people headed to Corfu, Greece, at the height of the summer season.

ABOVE: Britain's Home Office Minister David Mellor peers into wartorn Afghanistan from neighboring Pakistan as the Soviet war in the central Asian country continues.

1985

LEFT: American tennis player Anne White sports an all-in-one white catsuit at the 1985 Wimbledon tournament. The catsuit caused great deal of distraction and the umpire asked her to change during a delay in play.

OPPOSITE: Bond Girls attend the premiere of *A View to a Kill*, the 14th big screen outing for James Bond. The movie sees the British spy attempting to save Silicon Valley from the menacing intentions of the evil industrialist Max Zorin (Christopher Walken) and his tough sidekick Mayday (Grace Jones). *A View to a Kill* was the seventh and last time that Roger Moore would reprise his role as Bond.

1985

ᵗᵛ NEWS 2

SCHNEIDER X 3,7

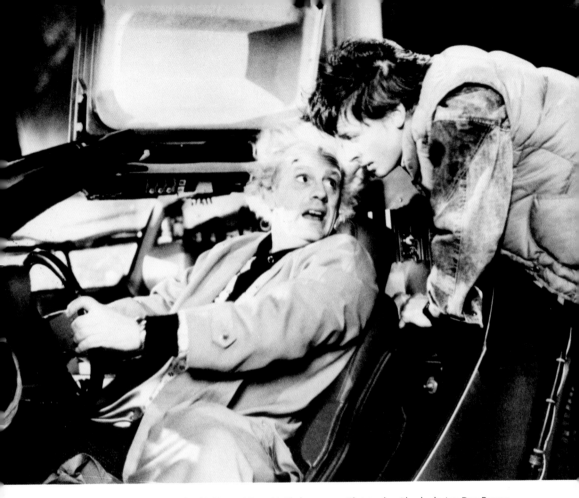

ABOVE: Michael J. Fox as Marty McFly leans over Christopher Lloyd, playing Doc Brown, who sits in the DeLorean car that was the time travel machine in sci-fi adventure movie *Back to the Future*. The movie was rated number 10 in the American Film Institute's top 10 sci fi films of all time and inspired a generation with the franchise that ran with two sequels.

OPPOSITE: Andrew Harvey, Julia Somerville, and John Humphrys, BBC newsreaders on the *Nine o'Clock News*.

RIGHT: Status Quo hit the charts with "Pictures of Matchstick Men" in 1967 and have rocked around the world ever since. However, 1985 was a difficult year for the band as founder member Alan Lancaster, who had left the band, took exception to developments and from his distant location in Australia and began legal proceedings, which were resolved in an out-of-court settlement in 1986 that allowed the new lineup to continue recording.

OPPOSITE: Princess Diana compensates Prince Charles with a kiss after his team were beaten in a championship polo match at Cowdray Park in Sussex.

ABOVE: Jerry Hall puts the finishing touches to Angelica Huston's makeup during Fashion Aid, the fashion world's contribution to tackling the famine in Ethiopia. Huston and Hall were joined by scores of models, celebrities, and politicians in raising money and awareness about the plight of the starving.

OPPOSITE: Freddie Mercury backstage at the Fashion Aid show with his best friend and onetime girlfriend Mary Austin. Mercury released his first solo album, *Mr. Bad Guy*, in April 1985. It included the song "I Was Born to Love You," which peaked at number 10 in the UK, but lacked the commercial success he was accustomed to with Queen.

1985

ABOVE: An explosion rips through a Royal Jordanian ALIA Boeing 727 at Beirut Airport in June 1985. The hijackers, linked to Hezbollah, allowed their hostages to escape before detonating the explosives they had left behind.

OPPOSITE: Terry Waite is escorted by the Lebanese army to his flight at Beirut Airport. Waite, an envoy of the Church of England and a veteran hostage negotiator, managed to secure the release of several hostages before being taken prisoner himself. He was held hostage for more than four and a half years, spending much of that time in solitary confinement.

1985

OPPOSITE: Hare coursing on the Oxfordshire estate of the Duke of Marlborough. Traditionally grayhounds were bred for the sport, which came to an end in 2005 following campaigning by anti-blood sports lobbyists.

RIGHT: Denis Thatcher, the husband of Brtain's Prime Minister, celebrates his putt with a Michael Jackson-style hip swinging gyration at a celebrity pro-am golf tournament.

1985

RIGHT: George Michael and Andrew Ridgeley, together pop duo Wham!, had their first international hit with "Wake Me up Before You Go-Go" in 1984. The pair had a busy year in 1985, first staging a groundbreaking tour of China, then taking part in Live Aid, and later releasing a new hit single, "I'm Your Man."

OPPOSITE: George Michael shows he does have rhythm on the dance floor.

1985

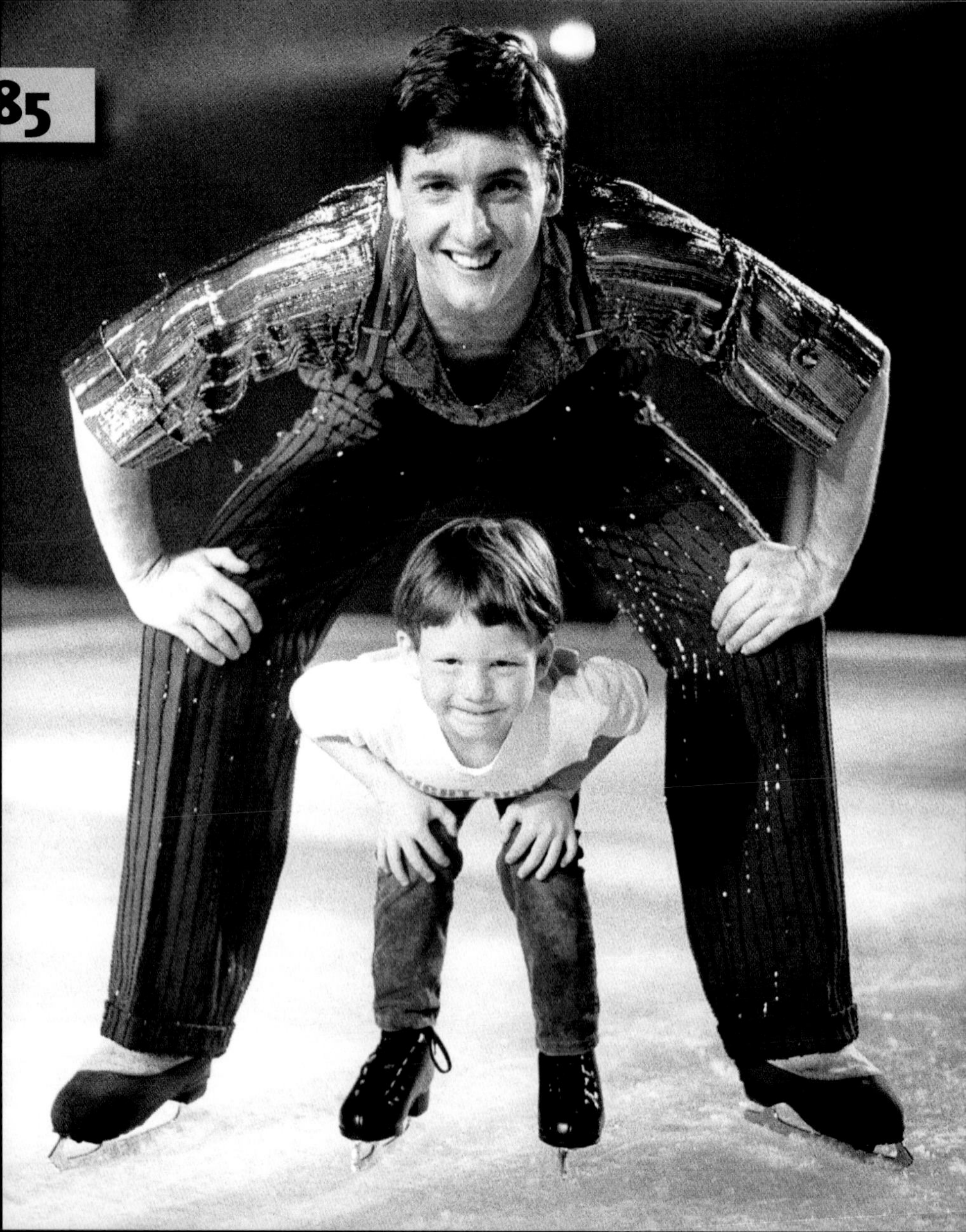

RIGHT: A Tamil Tiger guerrilla drapes himself with bullets before going out on patrol in a truck modified to take a mounted heavy-calibre machine gun. The Liberation Tigers of Tamil Eelam (LTTE) were a formidable separatist organization fighting for an independent Tamil state in its Sri Lankan homeland.

OPPOSITE: Ice skater Robin Cousins poses with his son, Robin Cousins Junior, on the ice in August 1985. Cousins Senior won Olympic and European Championship gold medals and in 1985 he was achieving back flip-triple toe-loop combinations in practice. In 1986 he famously performed two consecutive layout back flips in competition.

1986

US space shuttle *Challenger* lifts off on January 28, 1986, from a launchpad at Kennedy Space Center, just before it exploded, tragically killing its crew of seven. Media coverage of the mission was intense as non-NASA passenger Christa McAuliffe, the first member of the Teacher in Space project, was on board. NASA grounded the shuttle for more than two years while they reviewed all aspects of the technical data and proceedures surrounding the shuttle and in September 1988 the new shuttle *Discovery* was launched.

1986

LEFT: The cast of *Cheers*, the popular NBC TV comedy series set in a Boston bar, that ran for 11 seasons from 1982 to 1993. One of the show's characters, psychiatrist Dr. Frasier Crane (Kelsey Grammer), "moved back" to Seattle to feature in his own successful spin-off, *Frasier*. Shelley Long, Ted Danson, and Woody Harrelson all had successful Hollywood careers after leaving the show.

OPPOSITE: Microsoft founder and owner Bill Gates poses outdoors with Microsoft's first laptop in 1986 at the new 40-acre corprorate campus in Redmond, Washington. In March, Microsoft held an initial public offering of 2.5 million shares. By the end of the year, Gates became a billionaire at the age of 31. Microsoft was the first company to dominate the personal computer market with its MS-DOS operating system and subsequently the Windows operating platform, ushering in the mouse, a feature first made popular by Apple.

1986

RIGHT: Clint Eastwood produced, directed, and starred in the 1986 military drama *Heartbreak Ridge* about a US Marine sergeant leading a squadron of rookies into battle in Grenada. Eastwood played the hard-nosed, hard-living sergeant trying to lick the undisciplined young recruits into shape.

OPPOSITE: Duran Duran singer Simon Le Bon poses for photographers with his partner, model Yasmin Parvaneh, at the *Elle* magazine launch. The pair married two months later. Duran Duran had hits throughout the 1980s including "Notorious," "Rio," and the theme to the James Bond film *A View to a Kill*.

OPPOSITE: British Prime Minister Margaret Thatcher opened the final stretch of the M25 motorway, which forms a circle around London, in October 1986. Built to relieve London from the congestion arising from the huge increase in motor vehicles converging on the capital, often routing through the center to get to a destination on the other side of the city, it was not long before the M25 became the butt of English humor as it became congested and required widening. It is sometimes referred to as the world's biggest parking lot!

LEFT: On March 19, 1986, Buckingham Palace announced the engagement of the Queen's second son, Prince Andrew, to Sarah Ferguson. The pair were married four months later at Westminster Abbey and were given the titles Duke and Duchess of York.

1986

OPPOSITE: Brazilian Ayrton Senna leads Brit Nigel Mansell at the Monaco Formula One Grand Prix, where the two great rivals finished third and fourth respectively, with Alain Prost crossing the line first. Prost went on to win the 1986 Drivers' Championship, two points ahead of Mansell, who scooped second by one point from Nelson Piquet. Senna finished the season in fourth place.

LEFT: Alex Ferguson meets the players as he arrives for his first training session as the new manager of Manchester United in November 1986. That season United finished 11th, but Ferguson slowly managed to turn the club's fortunes around and it has been a dominant force in English football ever since.

Infielder Ray Knight of the
New York Mets is safe at first
base, beating the throw to
first baseman Bill Buckner
(right) of the Boston Red Sox
in a 1986 World Series game
in October, at Fenway Park.
The Mets won the series four
games to three, with Knight
scoring the winning run of
game six. Knight stepped into
the limelight in 1979 when
he replaced Pete Rose at the
Cincinnati Reds. He joined
the Mets in 1984.

1986

LEFT: In 1986 Halle Berry became the first African American to represent the United States at the Miss World competition. Berry, who was placed sixth, went on to have a successful acting career, winning the Best Actress Oscar for her performance in *Monster's Ball* in 2001.

OPPOSITE: Richard Branson proudly displays Virgin's latest share price outside one of his record stores. Always game for an adventure, Branson smashed the record for the fastest ever transatlantic crossing in his high-speed powerboat, the *Virgin Atlantic Flyer*, in June 1986. Although he shaved more than two hours off the previous record, Branson was not awarded the "Blue Riband" because his craft did not have a commercial purpose.

1986

RIGHT: Czech-born US tennis ace Martina Navratilova won her fifth consecutive Wimbledon Women's Singles title in 1986, defeating Czechoslovakia's Hana Mandlikova in the final. Earlier in the year she won the US Open by defeating another former compatriot, Helena Sukova.

OPPOSITE: William "the Refrigerator" Perry takes on Glen Titensor as the Chicago Bears storm past the Dallas Cowboys with a 17–6 victory. That year the Bears went all the way to the Super Bowl, defeating the New England Patriots 46–10 in the Louisiana Superdome in New Orleans.

OPPOSITE: Boris Becker, the youngest ever Wimbledon Men's Singles Champion, defends his title at his second Wimbledon Championship during the Men's Final against world number one Ivan Lendl in 1986. Eighteen-year-old Becker beat Lendl in straight sets, making Becker the 100th Men's Singles Champion.

RIGHT: Boris Becker jubilantly displays the Wimbledon Singles cup after winning on Centre Court.

1986

LEFT: Princess Stephanie of Monaco unveils her latest swimwear collection. The Princess turned to fashion after recovering from the crash that tragically killed her mother, Princess Grace.

OPPOSITE: John Taylor of Duran Duran. Although Andy Taylor and Roger Taylor had left the band, the three remaining Duran Duran members re-formed for the 1986 *Notorious* album. They continued to record and tour throughout the 1990s with new guitarist Warren Cuccurullo.

1986

OPPOSITE: Following on from the hugely successful 1984 movie *Purple Rain*, Prince returned to the big screen in *Under the Cherry Moon* in 1986. The movie, which Prince also directed, sees him playing a golddigger who falls in love with the young French heiress he is trying to swindle.

RIGHT: Prince in concert during his 1986 Parade tour, promoting his latest album *Parade*, which was the soundtrack from his movie *Under the Cherry Moon*. Starting out in London's Wembley Arena in August, the tour took in Europe and Japan, ending in Yokohama on September 9. This would be his last tour with backing band The Revolution. The album narrowly missed the top spot on both sides of the Atlantic but hit single "Kiss" charted at number one in the USA.

1986

LEFT: Whitney Houston's self-titled debut album became America's best-selling album of 1986. Critically acclaimed, it included hits "How Will I Know," "Greatest Love of All," and "Saving All My Love for You."

OPPOSITE: Eight years after her split from Ike, Tina Turner once again found international success with her album *Private Dancer*. Released in 1984, it included the hit "What's Love Got to Do With It," which was Turner's first solo US number one single.

1986

In 1986 Jack Nicklaus
capped his career by
recording his sixth
Masters victory. At 46, he
became the oldest Masters
winner in history. The
victory was his 18th major
title as a professional and
the last in his long career
on the PGA Tour. At the
age of 58, Nicklaus made
another run at the 1998
Masters, where eventually
he tied in sixth place.

1986

ABOVE: A victorious Liverpool team pose with the FA Cup in 1986 after defeating Everton by three goals to one at Wembley.

OPPOSITE: At the 1986 British Formula One Grand Prix, Belgian Thierry Boutsen's crash at the starting grid ended the race for him and the Formula One career of rising star Jacques Laffite, who suffered appalling leg injuries. The track was completely blocked by the many cars involved. The restart enabled Nigel Mansell, who had suffered a driveshaft failure during the original start, to switch cars and go on to win the race in a field depleted to only nine cars

ABOVE: Coming-of-age drama *Dirty Dancing*, starring Patrick Swayze and Jennifer Grey, was made as a low budget film with no major stars but became a surprise box office hit and has gone on to be a best selling video and DVD. Following his breakthrough role in *Dirty Dancing*, Swayze became typecast and starred in several unsuccessful movies, until his major 1990 hit *Ghost*, in which he played opposite Demi Moore. In 2009 Swayze died of pancreatic cancer.

OPPOSITE: Christopher Reeve in a scene from the 1987 film *Superman IV: The Quest for Peace*, his final movie in the highly successful series, based on the characters from the D.C. comics, which began in 1978.

1987

ABOVE: Mickey Rourke starred in the 1987 supernatural thriller *Angel Heart* alongside Robert De Niro and Lisa Bonet. Rourke made a succession of movies using his bad-boy looks, including the erotic *9 1/2 Weeks*, in which he starred opposite Kim Basinger.

OPPOSITE: Formula One star Ayrton Senna prepares to race during his third, and last, season at Lotus. Senna's fearless style of driving excited Formula One fans but many were uneasy about the risks he took. As Lotus's performance fell behind their Honda-powered opponents, Senna set his sights on the MacLaren team and would join Alain Prost there for the 1988 season.

The Untouchables, based on the 1959 television series of the same name, starred Kevin Costner, Robert De Niro, Sean Connery, and Andy Garcia. The movie was nominated for four Academy Awards, Sean Connery winning Best Actor in a Supporting Role.

1987

OPPOSITE: Syrian soldiers police West Beirut after Shi'ite Amal militia besieged the Shatila Palestinian refugee camp. Syrian President Assad carefully monitored and sponsored the fighting between rival Muslim groups in Lebanon: the Palestinians were mainly Sunni while Assad was Alawi, a Shi'a sect. Assad was deeply concerned that the PLO, using Lebanon as a base for raids on Israel, would force Syria into further conflict with Israel and also with their strong Sunni mission would destabilize his position in Syria. The presence of Syrian troops in Lebanon was to control the removal of Palestinians from Lebanon. During the so-called War of the Camps, there was intensive fighting and even artillery shelling as the Palestinians fought desperately to hold their positions against the Amal militia.

LEFT: A local resident shows his appreciation of the Syrian presence.

1987

RIGHT: Women campaign for equal rights to employment opportunities outside the Labour Party Conference in Brighton. The banners demand one woman be short-listed for every job opportunity.

OPPOSITE: The *Herald of Free Enterprise* ferry capsized after departure from the Channel port of Zeebrugge, Belgium, on a nighttime sailing in early March 1987. The tragedy cost the lives of 193 passengers and crew and resulted from the ferry's bow loading doors being left open, allowing water to flood in and turn the craft over on its side. When the electrics failed the ship was in total darkness and many deaths were caused by passengers unable to find an escape route while trapped in very cold water. The public inquiry laid blame on three of the ship's officers but also castigated the ship's owners.

1987

OPPOSITE: Diego Maradona evades a lunging tackle from Irish International Paul McGrath during the 1987 Football League Centenary match at Wembley Stadium which saw a Football League XI playing a World XI. The world side was captained by Maradona, making his first major appearance in England since the infamous "hand of God" incident in the quarter-finals of the World Cup in Mexico in 1986, when the talented Argentinian scored an illegal goal against England by punching the ball into the net with his hand.

LEFT: Australian tennis player Pat Cash won his one and only Grand Slam at Wimbledon in June 1987. Earlier in the year he finished as runner-up in his home country at the Australian Open, when he lost a tough five set match to Swedish Stefan Edberg.

OPPOSITE: Griff Rhys Jones gives direction to Mel Smith; together they were Britain's most successful comedy partnership since Morecambe and Wise. *Alas Smith and Jones* ran on the BBC for 60 shows over 10 seasons, from 1982 to 1998. Between series three and four, in 1987, they took *The World According to Smith and Jones* to London Weekend Television—a move that didn't endear them to the BBC. In 1981 the duo formed a management company, Talkback Productions, which produced some of Britain's most popular comedy shows of the 1980s and 1990s.

RIGHT: Lee Brown, son of circus entertainers at Sir Robert Fossett's Circus, pictured with his pal Dum Dum the elephant at the winter quarters in Northampton, in 1987. The Fossett family was England's oldest circus dynasty and it was said at one time that there was a Fosset in every circus in Britain.

ABOVE: US President Ronald Reagan and Soviet Premier Mikhail Gorbachev shake hands having signed the Intermediate-Range Nuclear Forces Treaty (INF) in Washington in December 1987—a clear indicator that the Cold War was coming to an end. Discussions leading to the INF Treaty began in 1980 and culminated just over 10 years later when the provisions of the Treaty were effected, with the destruction of nearly 3,000 medium range ballistic missiles.

OPPOSITE: The British Parliament passed the Channel Tunnel Act in 1987, agreeing to the construction of the underground link between Britain and France. Here Alistair Morton, the chairman of Eurotunnel, inspects the engineering work.

1987

RIGHT: Seventeen-year-old German tennis player Steffi Graf emerged on the scene in 1987 when she won her first Grand Slam title by beating Martina Navratilova on clay in the final of the French Open. Her successful year continued when she claimed the number one ranking that had previously belonged to her Czech-American opponent.

OPPOSITE: One of the most successful and prolific winners of the open era of tennis, Martina Navratilova loses her footing while playing Chris Evert-Lloyd in the Wimbledon semi final in 1987. The volatile, powerful, left-handed athlete had many hard-fought matches against her more composed American rival.

OPPOSITE: The measures taken by the British government to suppress the memoirs of retired MI5 officer Peter Wright led to many bizarre events. Though the ban in England covered both sale and press reporting, the court injunction did not apply in Scotland, where the book was on sale and freely reviewed in the media. The efforts of Tony Benn and others championing freedom of speech led to a lifting of the ban in 1987. Here Mrs. Joan Russell, who won a copy of *Spycatcher* in a raffle at London's Speakers' Corner, is talking to Tony Benn who had been publicly reading extracts from the controversial book.

LEFT: Colonel Oliver North testifies before a US Joint Congressional Committee established to ascertain the facts surrounding the Iran-Contra Affair. North was involved in funding the right-wing Contra rebels in Nicaragua with money covertly made by selling arms to Iran, ostensibly in the hope of securing the release of American hostages being held in Lebanon by Iranian-sponsored Shi'ite groups.

EDINBURGH
SPY
CATCHER
The Candid Autobiography of a
Intelligence Officer
WRIGHT
WRIGHT

1987

RIGHT: On her first world tour in 1987, which kicked off in Japan, a scantily clad Madonna wows audiences with her Who's That Girl tour. Between June and September 1987 the Queen of Pop performed in eight countries over three different continents. Her complex stage show involved seven costume changes and she performed songs from her latest album, *True Blue,* and the soundtrack of *Who's That Girl*, the movie in which she starred along with Griffin Dunne and John Mills.

OPPOSITE: British police officers surround

1987

A915 SYO

1987

RIGHT: British Formula One driver Nigel Mansell poses with his young passenger prior to winning the British Grand Prix at Silverstone. Driving well and in a great car, Mansell had bad luck during the season, which left him in second place behind teammate Nelson Picquet in the Drivers' Championship. However, in an amazing performance, Mansell won the British Grand Prix from a position 20 seconds behind the race leader, taking the checkered flag with his car virtually out of fuel.

OPPOSITE: Paul Newman takes a quick break from promoting his new film *The Color of Money*, a belated sequel to his 1961 movie *The Hustler*. Newman reprised his role as pool shark "Fast" Eddie Felton, who takes a gifted young pool player (Tom Cruise) under his wing in the hope of hustling more people. The film earned Newman the Best Actor Oscar at the 59th Academy Awards in 1987.

ABOVE: Pakistani opposition leader Benazir Bhutto marries businessman Asif Ali Zardari in December 1987. After Bhutto's assassination in 2007, Zardari took over as leader of his wife's political party and became President of Pakistan the following year.

OPPOSITE: Two-year-old Prince Harry plays on the bank of the River Dee under the watchful eye of his mother, Princess Diana during the royal family's summer break at Balmoral in 1987.

1987

OPPOSITE: Prince Charles has a passion for painting and is a keen amateur artist. Highgrove House, his Gloucestershire country home, contains many of his works—generally landscape paintings of royal estates or scenes from his extensive travels.

RIGHT: Rolling Stones guitarist Ronnie Wood attended Ealing College of Art in London before he embarked on his musical career. He maintained his love of art throughout his time as a rock musician and now paints and owns an art gallery with his sons.

1987

OPPOSITE: In June 1987 iconic movie actress Brigitte Bardot sold a collection of her personal possessions by auction in Paris. Bardot needed the money to fund her animal protection foundation. Over 2,000 fans attending the auction gave her a five minute standing ovation when she came on stage to open the event. The catalogue included everything from her guitar and makeup bag to a Cartier diamond bracelet; a Paco Rabanne metal mesh dress (shown here) fetched $3,900. The final item auctioned was not in the sale list: the auctioneer sold his own gavel, which he said he couldn't use any longer as it had ivory and whalebone decoration. It sold for $2,800.

LEFT: Top British swimmer Sharron Davies models fitness equipment in a fashionable leotard.

1987

ABOVE: Paul McCartney films a video for his new single "Once Upon a Long Ago," taken from his compilation album *All the Best!* The retrospective album went back as far as Paul's early solo career in 1970. The lineup for the single included wife Linda on keyboards, and a violin solo from virtuoso Nigel Kennedy. The video, like the single, drew on nostalgia for things of the past in an obvious pitch for a Christmas number one, but McCartney was beaten to the coveted spot by the Pet Shop Boys in the UK and George Michael in the US.

OPPOSITE: Janet Jackson's album *Control* was a big hit, awarded a Grammy for Album of the Year. Jackson's success with the album was significantly aided by her outstanding music videos which wowed MTV and its audience; much of the spectactular choreography was the work of Paula Abdul, at the time a yet-to-be-discovered artist.

1987

ABOVE: Pakistani cricket captain Imran Khan led his team to the semifinals of the 1987 Cricket World Cup. Kahn retired from cricket at the end of the competition, but rejoined the national team less than a year later at the request of the President of Pakistan, General Zia. While cricket might be his first love, Khan managed to find time to play the field with the ladies, many of whom developed an interest in cricket in an attempt to make a catch. Here he is photographed with 1970s supermodel Marie Helvin; he married Jemima Goldsmith in 1995.

OPPOSITE: David Bowie in concert in Rotterdam's Feijenoord Stadium in May, where his 1987 Glass Spider tour kicked off in support of his latest album *Never Let Me Down*. This tour surpassed the 1983 Serious Moonlight tour, with an estimated audience figure of three million and 86 performances around the world. Peter Frampton, iconic pop star of the 1960s, joined the band for the tour.

1987

ABOVE: Iranian troops man a position along the front lines facing Iraqi forces. For some time the Iraq–Iran War had reached a stalemate. With trench warfare and Iraq's use of chemical weapons the conflict was reminiscent of World War I. However, the stalemate of the land forces pushed both sides to increase strategic aerial strikes against the civilian populations, particularly in Tehran and Baghdad. When Iraq changed its frontline strategy from defensive to offensive, Iranian forces were overwhelmed, leading to Iran accepting a UN brokered cease-fire in summer 1988.

OPPOSITE: Frantic scenes on the trading floor as stocks crashed around the world on "Black Monday," October 19, 1987. The Dow Jones fell by more than 20 percent in just one day, leading to fears that the good times were over. However, the recovery was relatively quick and the 1980s economic boom rolled into the 1990s.

1987

OPPOSITE AND ABOVE: Exhausted firemen recuperate after battling a severe fire, which started when a flash fire engulfed an old wooden escalator at King's Cross Underground Station in London in November 1987. More than 150 firefighters wearing breathing apparatus tackled the blaze and searched for survivors but 31 people were killed and many more were injured. The fire started as the evening rush hour was trailing off but hundreds of commuters were trapped underground in one of London's busiest stations.

OPPOSITE AND RIGHT: Kylie Minogue and Jason Donovan both joined the cast of Australian soap *Neighbours* in 1986; the show first went on air in 1985 and failed to build the expected audience. The addition of the new younger cast members was heavily publicized, with the Minogue and Donovan characters in a focal romantic relationship. At a promotional event with fellow cast members, Minogue performed a couple of songs, including the Little Eva hit "Loco-Motion" as an encore. This led to a recording contract for Kylie and a local hit in Australia with "Loco-Motion" as her debut single. The following year she signed up with the British Stock, Aitken & Waterman songwriting and production team. Jason Donovan followed Kylie's trail to Stock, Aitken & Waterman in 1988, after his own first hit charted at number five in the UK. Having spiced up *Neighbours*, both actors departed the show in 1988 and 1989 respectively.

1988

OPPOSITE: Michael Jackson performs at Wembley Stadium in front of the Prince and Princess of Wales. He presented Diana, a Jackson fan, with specially engraved CDs of his hit albums *Bad* and *Thriller* and provided the Prince's Trust with a £150,000 check from his tour sponsors Pepsi.

RIGHT: Christian Bale and his sister Louise pictured at the London premiere of the Spielberg film *Empire of the Sun* in April 1988. The movie had its US release in December 1987 and won faint critical praise, though Bale's performance as Jim Graham was singled out as extraordinary (4,000 actors were auditioned for Bale's role). Receiving six nominations at the Academy Awards ceremony in 1988, the movie failed to win any. *Empire of the Sun* was the first of what would be a series of war movies by Spielberg that tried to make the experience of war a vivid reality to 'ordinary viewers', aided by the visual effects created by Industrial Light & Magic to recreate historical situations instead of fantasy.

ABOVE: Tom Cruise plays opposite Dustin Hoffman in *Rain Man*. The film, directed by Barry Levinson, explores the relationship of two estranged brothers, with Hoffman playing the autistic savant opposite Cruise's unscrupulous entrepreneur. Swinging between comedy and pathos, the movie leaves the audience up in the air after a rollercoaster moral journey. *Rain Man* received four Academy Awards, incuding Best Picture and Best Actor in a Leading Role for Dustin Hoffman's portrayal of Raymond Babbitt.

OPPOSITE: Linford Christie, part of Britain's sprint relay squad, pictured with his Olympic medal.

OPPOSITE: Matt and Luke Goss, identical twins and two thirds of boy band Bros, appear on stage during their 1988 Big Push tour. The third member of the British group was their school friend Craig Logan. The band had 11 top 40 singles and three top 20 albums in the UK before they broke up in 1992.

RIGHT: Front man Bono and guitarist The Edge of Irish rock band U2. They achieved their first UK number one in 1988 with their song "Desire." *Rattle and Hum*, the documentary that followed their 1987 Joshua Tree tour, gave U2 a number one album based on the film and with the same name.

ABOVE: Robbie Coltrane and David Jason are a pair of versatile thespians known for playing comedic and straight roles. Both were nominated for the 1988 BAFTA Award for Best Actor—Jason won for his performance as the head porter of a fictional Cambridge college in the adaptation of Tom Sharpe's novel *Porterhouse Blue*, beating Coltrane who played a rotund rock star in the BBC series *Tutti Frutti*.

OPPOSITE: Steven Spielberg's *Empire of the Sun* was shot in Shanghai and Spain but with studio scenes filmed in England's Elstree Studios. Most would connect Spielberg with Hollywood, but the skills and facilities of Elstree were still in demand. Although the studios were in decline and continuously changing ownership at this time, with a substantial part of its backlot sold off to a major supermarket, it was the studio base for the first three *Star Wars* movies and the Indiana Jones trilogy, making Spielberg a regular at the studios.

1988

RIGHT: Newcastle midfielder Paul Gascoigne, a.k.a Gazza, tussles with Wimbledon's John Fashanu shortly before his transfer to Tottenham Hotspur for a record-breaking £2.3 million. Under the adroit manager Terry Venables, the headstrong Geordie blossomed into an international class footballer and Gascoigne won his first England cap in September 1988.

OPPOSITE: Swede Stefan Edberg shows his appreciation of the Wimbledon Men's Singles cup after defeating Germany's Boris Becker in the 1988 final, which ran over two days when rain interrupted the match. His first Wimbledon title, it was also the first of three consecutive Wimbledon finals in which Edberg faced Becker, who beat the Swede in straight sets the following year, with Edberg winning the five-set final in 1990.

1988

Canadian sprinter Ben Johnson
(second from left) wins the
final of the 100 meters at the
Olympic Games in Seoul,
South Korea, 1988. Scandal
surrounded Johnson after
he won the event in a world
record time of 9.79 seconds,
but was later disqualified for
doping. Carl Lewis (far right) of
the USA took the gold.

RIGHT: The outspoken American-born comedienne Ruby Wax started her showbiz career as a straight actress before her appearances in various British TV programs showcased her brash up-front personality and opened the door for her own show. In *Ruby's Celebrity Bash,* she found her niche as an interviewer who delivered hilarious one-liners with alacrity.

OPPOSITE: Benazir Bhutto tries to relax as she awaits the results of the first free elections in Pakistan for more than a decade. The November 1988 vote saw the Pakistan Peoples Party win a majority in the National Assembly and Bhutto was sworn in as the country's first female prime minister one month later.

OPPOSITE: Professional tennis player Gabriella Sabatini tries her hand at Real Tennis. The accomplished Argentinian athlete had teamed up with Steffi Graf to win the Women's Doubles title at Wimbledon before competing in the 1988 Seoul Summer Olympics, where she won the silver medal in the Women's Singles—beaten to into second place by her German Wimbledon doubles partner!

RIGHT: Prince Charles and Princess Diana dance together on a tour of Thailand and Australia in 1988. In January Australia began its bicentennial celebrations and in February the King of Thailand hosted the royal couple on the occasion of his 60th birthday.

ABOVE AND OPPOSITE: President Reagan paid a formal visit to London in June 1988, returning from the historic Moscow summit with Soviet President Mikhail Gorbachev that ratified INF treaty and discussed further rapprochement between the US and Russia under the new policies of *glasnost* and *perestroika*. Reagan delivered a speech to members of the Royal Institute of International Affairs at the Guildhall, where he proclaimed a "new era in history," heralding the end of the Cold War. Reagan's cordial remarks about Prime Minister Thatcher and the British role in NATO marked a high point in the special relationship between the two nations. Reagan was conscious of the ending of his second term of presidency, which had overseen momentous changes in the world.

World Heavyweight Boxing Champion Mike Tyson sits next to new manager Don King in Chicago, Illinois, in December 1988. Two years earlier Tyson had become the youngest WBC heavyweight champion in history when he knocked out defending champion Trevor Berbick in his first title fight. 1988 was a turbulent year for Tyson: he also changed his long-standing trainer, Kevin Rooney, leading to Tyson's focus less on craft and more on the style that succeeded in his title fight with Michael Spinks, who he knocked out after 91 seconds in June that year, considered by some to be the pinnacle of Tyson's career in the ring.

1988

ABOVE: Syrian troops are deployed in Southern Beirut to support the Lebanese Amal militia. Amal was fighting the pro-Iranian Hezbollah for control of the southern suburbs, where many Western hostages, including the humanitarian Terry Waite, were being held.

OPPOSITE: Hezbollah and Iranian guards retreat to their last stronghold, the "Hostage Hilton." Anglican envoy Terry Waite went to Beirut in January 1987 to negotiate the release of several hostages, including John McCarthy, Terry Anderson, and Tom Sutherland. However, Waite was himself taken hostage by a group of Hezbollah Shi'ite Muslims and held in captivity for 1,763 days.

1988

LEFT: Michael Douglas won the Academy Award for Best Actor for his role as the unscrupulous broker Gordon Gekko in Oliver Stone's movie *Wall Street* in 1988. The movie, a tale of corporate greed and intrigue, was topical for the maverick market growth of the 1980s and a sequel is currently being mooted, again directed by Stone, with the recent world financial crisis making it a timely production.

OPPOSITE: Young Welsh actress Catherine Zeta-Jones gets her first big break, starring in the West End musical *42nd Street*. Zeta-Jones had trained for the musical stage and when the lead and her understudy fell sick, Catherine took the starring role. Her career made a step-change when she played coquettish Mariette in the 1991 TV series *The Darling Buds of May*.

1988

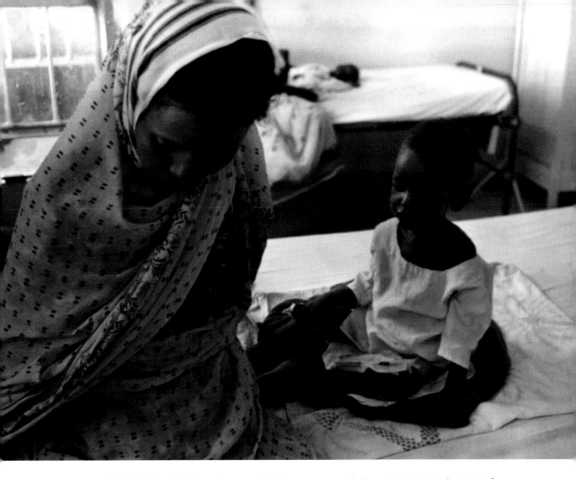

OPPOSITE: Monday, December 12, 1988: the scene near Clapham Junction, London, one of Europe's busiest stations, after a London-bound commuter train plowed into the back of a stationary train, killing 35 people and injuring hundreds more.

ABOVE: As if the 1988 famine in Sudan wasn't enough of a humanitarian disaster, the combination of drought conditions and the human rights abuses inflicted during the Second Sudanese Civil War were made even worse when heavy rainfall in August caused devastating flooding of the Blue Nile and the White Nile, affecting huge areas across Sudan.

1988

ABOVE: A convoy of Soviet armored personnel vehicles cross the bridge at Termez, Uzbekistan, at the Soviet–Afghan border during the withdrawal of the Red army from Afghanistan, May 1988. The so-called Afghanistan-Uzbekistan Friendship Bridge was built by the Russians in 1982 to facilitate the transport of their forces and material into Afghanistan.

OPPOSITE: Canadian hockey star Wayne Gretzky, nicknamed "the Great One," announcing his trade by the Edmonton Oilers to the LA Kings in August 1988. Acquiring Gretzky led to an immediate improvement in the Kings' performance, taking them to the top of the league and the popularizing of ice hockey in California. Winner of numerous trophies, Gretzky is widely credited as the greatest NHL player of all time and on his retirement in 1999 was immediately inducted into the Hockey Hall of Fame.

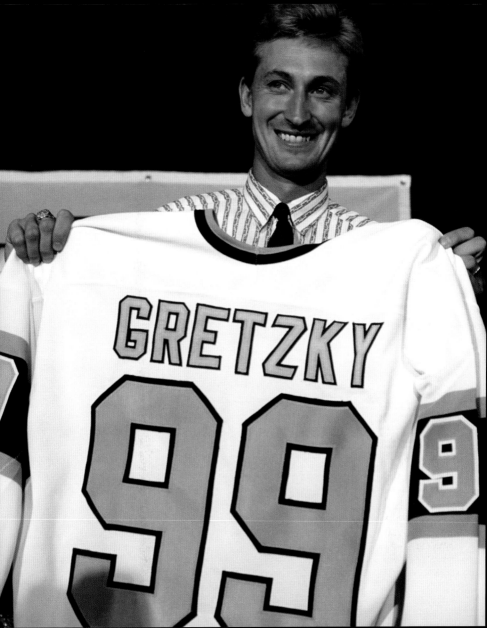

1988

RIGHT: Mick Jagger struts his stuff on stage during the Rolling Stones' Steel Wheels world tour. The album of the same name reached number one in the US and number two in the UK.

OPPOSITE: The Eurythmics, Dave Stewart and Annie Lennox, performing at the Nelson Mandela 70th Birthday Concert at Wembley Stadium on June 11, 1988. The concert, which also starred Sting, Dire Straits, Stevie Wonder, Whitney Houston, and the Bee Gees, was broadcast around the world, but not in South Africa. Harry Belafonte's introduction was intended to be the key appeal to the South African government to release Mandela, which eventually took place 20 months later, 27 years after Mandela had been incarcerated.

1988

OPPOSITE: Officers of the Metropolitan Police pictured wearing red noses during a press call in 1988 to promote Comic Relief's first ever Red Nose Day, inspired by the *Secret Policeman's Ball* events from 1976-1981 in aid of Amnesty International. The first Red Nose Day raised £15 million for charity and became a regular event backed by BBC Television, which hosts a telethon appeal every other year.

LEFT: Wheel clamping was an unpopular innovation in the 1980s and caused misery to miscreant parkers, sometimes unaware of the rules. Spirits were raised when Simon Hilton, who maintained the clamping computer, was himself clamped.

1988

OPPOSITE AND ABOVE: Police examine the wreckage of the Pan-Am 747 aircraft which crashed on the town of Lockerbie in Scotland on December 21, 1988. The plane had been en route from London's Heathrow to New York's John F. Kennedy International Airport when a bomb exploded, killing all 243 passengers and 16 crew members. Eleven people in Lockerbie were also killed when large sections of the plane fell in and around the town. In 2001, after finally being brought to trial in the Netherlands in 1999, Abdelbaset Ali Mohmed Al Megrahi, a Libyan, was convicted of involvement in the bombing and sentenced to life imprisonment in a Scottish jail. On August 20, 2009, the Scottish government released him on compassionate grounds to return to Libya since he

1988

OPPOSITE: Palestinian youths jeer at an Israeli soldier in the Nuseirat refugee camp in the Gaza Strip. Many Palestinians who took part in the Intifada (uprising) were youths who had spent their whole lives under the Israeli occupation. Between 1987 and 1993 it is estimated that 1,100 Palestinians were killed by Israeli forces and 160 Israelis killed by Palestinians. Many more Palestinians were killed by their own people for being collaborators.

RIGHT: Armed with catapults, young Palestinians fire marbles at Israeli troops following Friday prayers in the casbah of Nablus. Other weaponry used against Israelis included Molotov cocktails, hand grenades, and guns.

1989

ABOVE: One of New York's most celebrated attractions, the Rockefeller Center comprises 19 buildings and the iconic space pictured here—the Rockefeller Plaza, which here a spin-off from the US Open. In 1989, Japanese industrial giant Mitsubishi purchased the property in its entirety from the owners, the Rockefeller Group.

OPPOSITE: Heavyweight boxers Mike Tyson and Frank Bruno pose together. The pair fought in February 1989 and although Bruno started well, he was knocked out by Tyson in the fifth round.

PRESTO Engineers Cutting Tools

ABOVE: At the FA Cup semi-final tie between Liverpool and Nottingham Forest, a total of 95 Liverpool fans were killed when they were crushed in the West Stand of Sheffield Wednesday's stadium, which was overfilled by an influx of supporters eager to see the game; they had been delayed in entering the match, which was already several minutes in progress. The referee halted the game when he saw fans clambering over the barrier fence to escape the crush. After the fence collapsed the focus of the police was on keeping the opposing supporters separated. Following the tragedy, many safety regulations were enacted to avoid a future recurrence.

OPPOSITE: Floral tributes are laid by supporters outside the gates of the ground in the wake of the Hillsborough disaster.

1989

LEFT: British Foreign Secretary John Major stands outside the Foreign and Commonwealth Office shortly before he became Chancellor of the Exchequer in a cabinet reshuffle. He was not Chancellor for long, rising to party leader and then, in 1990, to Prime Minister after Margaret Thatcher's forced exit. He would remain at Number 10 until New Labour's landslide victory, headed by Tony Blair, in 1997.

OPPOSITE: President George Bush with his wife Barbara as they board *Air Force One*. It was Bush's first visit to Britain as President and he put particular emphasis on the "special relationship" between the two countries. Bush and Thatcher discussed the need to shift their policy toward the Soviet Union from military-backed standoff to peaceful economic interaction, in the wake of Gorbachev's reforms.

1989

San Francisco 49ers running back Roger Craig (number 33) is the first player to mob wide receiver John Taylor (number 82) after Taylor grabs the game-winning 10-yard touchdown pass from Hall of Fame quarterback Joe Montana with just 34 seconds remaining in Super Bowl XXIII, changing the 49ers' score of 16–13 down to a 20–16 victory over the Cincinnati Bengals on January 22, 1989, at Joe Robbie Stadium in Miami, Florida. Taylor was noted for his catching ability, aided by his enormous hands.

1989

LEFT: Annabel Croft (right), former tennis player and copresenter of TV challenge show *Treasure Hunt,* with sister Louisa (17) in London's Covent Garden. At the end of the final series of *Treasure Hunt,* Annabel was offered the role of host in new TV gameshow *Interceptor,* which was well received but only ran for one season.

OPPOSITE: Goth culture resurfaced in the late 1980s with emphasis upon customized leather jackets, pointed boots, and lots of crushed velvet.

Harrison Ford reprises his action hero role
of Indiana Jones in the 1989 sequel movie,
Indiana Jones and the Last Crusade. Ford and
Sean Connery, who plays Indiana's father,
battle against the Nazis in a quest for the
Holy Grail. *The Last Crusade* outgrossed
the previous two films in the Indiana Jones
franchise.

1989

Tom Cruise in the 1989 film adaptation of *Born on the Fourth of July*, which was based on the autobiography of Vietnam war veteran Ron Kovic. Here Cruise, in the role of Kovic, dances with his girlfriend the night before joining the Marines. Although it touched on many contentious issues relating to the Vietnam War and the treatment of veterans, Oliver Stone's movie was a critical and commercial success, winning two Academy Awards, four Golden Globes and a Directors' Guild of America Award. It also gave Cruise his first Academy Award nomination.

1989

RIGHT: Author Salman Rushdie holds a copy of his novel *The Satanic Verses*. Published in 1988, it was surrounded by controversy in the Islamic world due to Rushdie's perceived irreverence toward the Qu'ran and the Prophet Muhammad. The Muslim outcry reached its peak with the fatwa issued by Ayatollah Ruhollah Khomeini, the Supreme Leader of Iran, in February 1989, urging good Muslims to kill Rushdie and his publishers. Several translators became vicitims but Rushdie survived, receiving police protection from the UK government.

OPPOSITE: Almost fully submerged, River Thames pleasure-cruiser *The Marchioness* is pictured where it sank when the dredger *Bowbelle* collided with it in midstream, near Cannon Street railway bridge, during the night of October 19–20. The boat had been hired for a birthday party, attended by over 100 people. *The Marchioness* sank very rapidly, having been capsized by the fast-moving dredger, resulting in the deaths of 51 people.

ABOVE: Princes William and Harry, who are acting as pages for their uncle, greet the newly weds Charles Spencer and model Catherine Lockwood on September 16 at St. Mary's, Great Brington. Lord Spencer delivered the eulogy at the funeral service for his older sister Diana at Westminster Abbey, London, on September 6, 1997.

OPPOSITE: Latin American dance craze the Lambada made a wave around the world, reaching its peak in summer 1989 fueled by French band Kaoma's hit "Lambada," which sold five million copies worldwide.

OPPOSITE: In 1989 Bill Wyman married 18-year-old Mandy Smith, whom he had been dating since she was 13 and he was 47. Their relationship was the subject of considerable media attention. The marriage ended in spring 1991 but returned to media focus when Wyman's son by his first marriage started dating Mandy's mother Patsy in 1993, before Wyman Senior's decree nisi.

LEFT: Paul McCartney in concert in Drammen, near Oslo, Norway, on his eponymous world tour, which kicked off there in September 1989 and wound up in Chicago in July 1990. It was the former Beatle's first tour under his own name and included many Lennon-McCartney compositions in the set list. Wife Linda played keyboards on the tour.

1989

LEFT: By the 1980s, English blues-rock guitarist, singer, and composer Eric Clapton was established as one of the greatest guitarists of all time. In 1989 Clapton released *Journeyman*, an album encompassing a wide range of styles including blues, jazz, soul, and pop. The album title implies a certain modesty, reflecting Clapton's early reticence to sing lead vocals. *Journeyman* provided Eric with two US number one singles and a Grammy award, as well as being certified double platinum.

OPPOSITE: Phil Collins started his showbiz career as an actor and model but interest in music, and drumming in particular, led to his recruitment as a member of progressive rock group Genesis. He soon added lead vocals to his list of accomplishments, before turning his hand to record production. In 1989, Collins produced his successful album, ... *But Seriously*, which explored social themes such as homelessness, the subject of his worldwide number one single, "Another Day in Paradise."

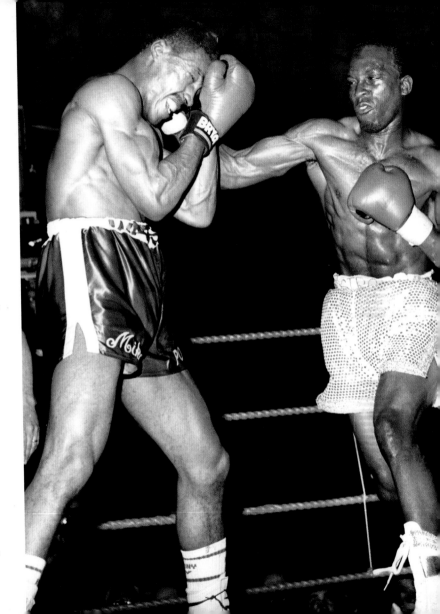

RIGHT: The highlight of Michael Watson's career was his thrilling May 1989 victory over Nigel Benn, securing him the British Commonwealth middleweight title. Watson beat the undefeated Benn in a sixth round knock-out in front of a sell-out crowd, which was packed into "The Super Tent" in Finsbury Park, London.

OPPOSITE: Boxer Muhammad Ali, formerly Cassius Clay, visits the past with his old opponents Joe Frazier and George Foreman to promote the new video release, *Champions Forever*, in 1989.

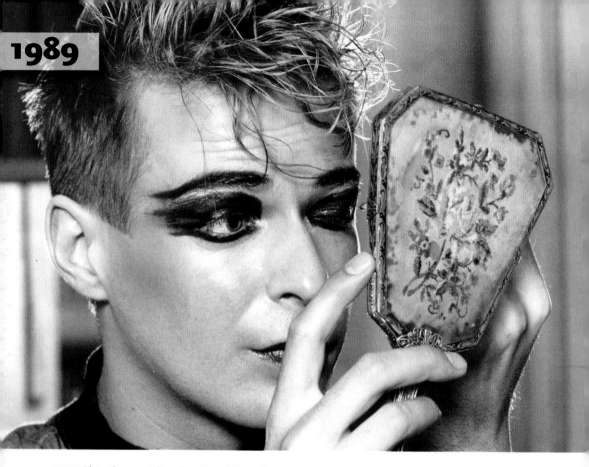

ABOVE: Blatantly camp Julian Clary started his performing career as a stand-up comic on the alternative comedy circuit. His performances soon led to him being given his own lighthearted game show, *Sticky Moments with Julian Clary*, on UK's Channel 4 TV—a platform that showcased Clary's outrageous brand of humor with its heavy reliance on innuendo and double entendre.

OPPOSITE: Her trademark long blond hair and commanding height ensure that leggy Texan supermodel Jerry Hall is one of the most photographed women in the world. Like her rock star partner, Mick Jagger, the cool blonde turned her hand to acting and in 1989 she appeared in a supporting role as Alicia Hunt, a gangster's moll disfigured by the Joker in Tim Burton's *Batman*.

ABOVE: After Nottingham Forest supporters invaded the pitch at the end of a turbulent League Cup quarter-final victory over Queen's Park Rangers in February 1989, Forest manager Brian Clough was also photographed on the pitch. The charismatic and outspoken manager was fined £5,000 for bringing the game into disrepute, and banned from the touchline of all Football League grounds for the rest of the season.

OPPOSITE: Fifteen-year-old tennis prodigy Monica Seles joined the full time professional tennis circuit in 1989 and won her first WTA singles title at the Virginia Slims Championships in Houston, when she beat seasoned champion Chris Evert in three sets.

E604 MAV

OPPOSITE: The Duke and Duchess of York head for the pistes. At a personal level, as this picture reveals, their relationship was entering a chilly spell, perhaps brought on by Andrew's regular naval postings taking him away from his wife and daughters for up to six months at a time. Sadly their romance moved on to a slippery slope in the early 1990s and they announced their formal separation in 1992.

ABOVE: Mrs. Thatcher uses the latest in urban cleansing to remove the plentiful evidence of those Downing Street pigeons. She shares the cab of the street-cleaning machine with Lady Porter, leader of Westminster City Council, who would be later implicated in a gerrymandering scandal behind the Conservative Party's landslide victory in London's 1990 local elections—a slightly different example of Thatcher's driving force.

RIGHT: Classical violinist Nigel Kennedy draws the crowds during an impromptu busking session. Kennedy's individualistic personal style and his crossover musicial disciplines enabled him to succeed in numerous genres—also to introduce a young generation to Vivaldi's *Four Seasons*, which was a giant hit for him and the English Chamber Orchestra in 1989.

OPPOSITE: In late 1989, Gloria Estefan released her best-selling album to date, *Cuts Both Ways*. While touring in support the album Estefan was critically injured, suffering a fractured spine when a speeding vehicle crashed into her tour bus in March 1990. Luckily, she completely recovered and returned to touring ten months after the accident.

1989

A lone demonstrator in a standoff with a column of tanks on June 5, 1989, at the entrance to Tiananmen Square, Beijing, in the People's Republic of China. The incident took place the morning after Chinese troops fired upon pro-democracy protesters who had been occupying the square since April 15. The act of bravery by the anonymous man in the photograph was captured by photographer Jeff Widener and syndicated to the world's press as a poignant symbol of the social and political struggle going on in China. The number of deaths resulting from the "Massacre" of June 4 remains unknown.

OPPOSITE: Pro-democracy students in China march on Tiananmen Square in Beijing to join 150,000 protesters demonstrating at the funeral of the sacked reformist politician, Hu Yao-Bang. The demonstration was brutally suppressed as the army opened fire on the protesters, killing a number estimated between several hundred and several thousand people, depending on the intelligence source. China drew widespread international condemnation, but this did little to counter the internal political reaction, which was to punish the leaders of this protest with imprisonment and even execution.

ABOVE: Women wearing a white rosette of mourning show their distress as reports of the Tiananmen massacre are relayed to members of Britain's Chinese community in Gerrard Street, the heart of London's Chinatown.

ABOVE: *Blackadder Goes Forth* is the satirical fourth and final series of the comedy starring Rowan Atkinson and Tony Robinson, Stephen Fry, Hugh Laurie, and Tim McInerny. This series was written by Richard Curtis and Ben Elton and was set on the Western Front of World WarI .

OPPOSITE: Meg Ryan shares a moment with Princess Diana at the London premiere of *When Harry Met Sally...* the film directed by Rob Reiner with screenplay by Nora Ephron. Ryan's co-star Billy Crystal looks on. The movie was a big box office success—its New York City backdrop and big band soundtrack, provided by Harry Connick, Jr. (winning him his first Grammy), combined to make the movie a convincing portrayal of the single life in 1980s.

1989

OPPOSITE: Houses on Fairlight Cliffs near Hastings are in danger of collapsing into the sea below. The sandstone and clay coastline is one of many areas in the world that are affected by the problem of coastal erosion.

ABOVE: Racehorse Desert Orchid is spurred on to another victory in his spectacular 1989 season by jockey Richard Dunwoody, winning his third King George VI Steeplechase at Kempton Park. But his most famous win that year was the Cheltenham Gold Cup, voted the best horse race ever by *Racing Post* readers. Affectionately known as Dessie, the courageous gray was one of the nation's favorite National Hunt racehorses, much loved for his front-running, attacking style.

OPPOSITE: Wreckage of the British Midland Boeing 737 aircraft which crashed on the MI motorway outside Kegworth in Leicestershire. The crash, which claimed 46 lives and left many of the 79 survivors badly injured, was caused by one of the plane's two engines malfunctioning and catching fire. An unfortunate sequence of events led the aircrew to shut down the wrong engine and the loss of power caused the plane to crash on the embankment of the M1.

ABOVE: The scene after a Horsham-to-London train was hit from behind by another train going from Littlehampton to London. The Littlehampton train careered down the embankment into gardens below. Following an investigation into the crash, which killed eight people, it was concluded that fault lay with the train's driver, Robert Morgan, who pleaded guilty to manslaughter.

1989

LEFT: West Berliners in the French sector look over the wall into East Berlin without fear of retribution. On November 9, 1989, the border separating West from East Germany was finally opened. Thousands of West Berliners gathered at the Brandenburg Gate, the heart of the divided city, and had a party on top of the Wall that had split Berlin since 1961.

OPPOSITE: The Berlin Wall was breached after nearly three decades following East Germany's Communist rulers gave permission for gates along the Wall to be opened. Euphoric crowds immediately began to clamber on top of the Wall and used chisels, screwdrivers, and improvised tools to break up the symbol of East—West division.

1989

OPPOSITE: East Germans line up to cross the border as they are allowed to travel freely directly to West Germany for the first time since the erection of the Berlin Wall in 1961. The Berlin Wall was 27 miles of concrete rampart that divided West Berlin from East Berlin, although much of the barrier actually consisted of wire fencing, supported by strict patrols and spotlight equipped watchtowers.

ABOVE: East German guards stand atop the Berlin Wall watching as a demonstrator waves a West German flag. From the time of its erection, around 5,000 people are thought to have successfully escaped across the Wall; however many of those who attempted to escape were shot dead by border guards.

1989

RIGHT: Born into an acting family, Julia Roberts made her movie debut opposite her brother Eric, but it was the 1988 movie *Mystic Pizza* that got her career rolling. In 1989 her portrayal of Shelby in tearjerker *Steel Magnolias* won her an Oscar nomination for Best Supporting Actress alongside veteran stars Sally Field, Dolly Parton, and Shirley MacLaine. But playing opposite Richard Gere in the 1990 movie *Pretty Woman* was the breakout role that made her a world-ranking star.

OPPOSITE: Naomi Campbell, fashion model, relaxes at home. Campbell was spotted at the age of 15 while shopping in London's Covent Garden. After signing up as a catwalk model she soon became in demand for brand campaigns such as Ralph Loren and, while still only 15, appeared on the cover of *Elle* magazine. At the time of this picture she was 19 and had already featured on several *Vogue* covers across the world and was on her way to being a household name.

1989

OPPOSITE: Military dictator of Panama Manuel Noriega talks to the press, denying claims that he rigged the election in 1989. According to the official government results, Carlos Duque (Noriega's handpicked candidate) won a landslide victory over the leading opposition candidate, Guillermo Endara, although the exit polls suggested otherwise.

ABOVE: Kashmiri separatist leader Shabir Shah leads a march in Srinagar in Indian-controlled Kashmir. Pakistan claimed the insurgency was being fueled by separatists from within Indian-controlled Kashmir. India argued that the insurgents were entering Kashmir from the outside with support from the Pakistani government.

1989

RIGHT: Romania's maverick socialist dictator Nicolai Ceausescu delivers his last speech from the balcony of the Communist Party Headquarters in Bucharest, December 21, 1989. A stunned Ceausescu was silenced as the crowd began jeering during his speech. By the end of the year, the dictator and his wife, Elena, would be sentenced to death and executed by firing squad.

OPPOSITE: The end of an era: a statue of Lenin is removed from what is now called Revolution Square in Bucharest. Although the National Salvation Front, which set up an interim government after Nicolae Ceausescu's removal, was made up of members of the Communist Party, it set Romania on a path to democracy and later EU membership, holding elections in 1990.

ACKNOWLEDGMENTS

Written and edited by
Tim Hill; Gareth Thomas; Murray Mahon; Marie Clayton; Duncan Hill; Jane Benn; Alison Gauntlett; Alice Hill.

****

The photographs in this book are from the archives of the *Daily Mail*. Thanks to all the photographers who have contributed and the film and television companies who have provided Associated Newspapers with promotional stills.
Every effort has been made to correctly credit photographs provided. In case of inaccuracies or errors we will be happy to correct them in future printings of this book.

Thanks to all the staff at Associated Newspapers who have made this book possible. Particular thanks to Alan Pinnock.
Thanks also to Steve Torrington, Dave Sheppard and Brian Jackson.

Thanks to the many Associated Newspapers photographers who have contributed including:
Monty Fresco, Michael Fresco, Ted Blackbrow, James Gray, Graham Wood, Bill Cross
Mike Forster, Neville Marrine, B Farrell, David Parker, Mike Hollist, Paul Lewis, Phillip Jackson, Alan Davidson, David Bennett, John Walters, Paul Fievez, Laurence Cottrell, Geoffrey Croft, Steve Back, Chris Barham, B Greenwood, Steve Bent, Geoffrey White, Phil Loftus, Frederic Neema, John Chapman, Malcolm Clarke, Dennis O' Regan, Graham Trott, Jon Hoffman, Adebari, David Katz, Adrian Brooks, Brendan Beirne, George Le Kerle, Derek Hawkins, William Lovelace, Steve Douglass, Denis Jones, Philip Ide, Steve Poole, Alex Yeung, Clive Lumpkin, David O'Neill, Jeremy Selwyn, Jim Hollander, Mark Richards, Darryn Lyons, Terry McGough, Barry Beattie, Steve Hodgson, Dave Crump, Lomas, David Stevens, Ian Turner, Aidan Sullivan, Postlethwaite, Arron, Alison McDougall, Alex Lentati, Frank Tewksbury, G. Copus, D. Benett, Keith Pannell,
With contributions from associated photographers: Mourad Raouf, Jamal, Ebet Roberts, Richard E. Aaron, Corbis, Vitaly Armand, Al Messerschmidt, Menahem Kahana, Abdul Rouf, Emil Houdek

Additional photographs courtesy Getty Images
Steve Powell, Getty Images North America pg 16-17; Stringer, Michael Ochs Archives, Getty Images pg 30-31; Getty Images North America pg 42-43; Focus on Sport/Getty Images pg 46-

Published by Transatlantic Press
First published in 2010

Transatlantic Press
38 Copthorne Road
Croxley Green, Hertfordshire
WD3 4AQ

© Atlantic Publishing
For photograph copyrights see pages 382–3

A catalogue record for this book is available from the British Library.

ISBN 978-1-907176-02-9

Printed in China